LOVING
FROM YOUR SOUL

Creating Powerful Relationships

SHEPHERD HOODWIN

Summerjoy Press
LAGUNA BEACH, CALIFORNIA
1995, 1997

Loving from Your Soul—Creating Powerful Relationships

PUBLISHED BY:
Summerjoy Press
31423 S. Coast Hwy. #84
Laguna Beach CA 92677-3056
(714) 499-3197
888-LIVE JOY (888-548-3569)

SummerjoyP@AOL.com
http://members.AOL.com/ShepherdH

DISTRIBUTED BY:
APG
1501 County Hospital Rd.
Nashville TN 37218
800-327-5113 East
800-275-2606 West

Printed in the United States of America on acid-free paper with soy-based ink.

ISBN 1-885469-02-0
Library of Congress Catalog Card Number 94-092317

99 98 97

15 14 13 12 11 10 9 8 7 6 5 4 3

Cover design by Melody Cassen.
Photograph of Shepherd Hoodwin by Billy Jim.

Dedicated to

Ruth Keller Hoodwin

The Loving Soul Who Was My Mother

ACKNOWLEDGMENTS

My clients, for their excellent questions,
and the use of material from their sessions.
Leslie-Anne Skolnik and **Pat Kendall,**
for editing and proofing.
Kent Babcock, Ed Hamerstrom, Shirley Nichols, and **Mayo Gray**, for additional feedback and suggestions.
Linda Scheurle, for excellent, accurate transcribing
of the majority of the material in this book.
Fay Goldie, Seth Cohn, Kent Babcock, Barry Carl,
and **Evelyn Jones,** for additional transcribing.
Billy Jim and **Richard Reed**, for taking the author photograph.
Sylvia Dweck, for generous gifts
of chicken soup and a computer.
Seth Cohn, for computer assistance.
Neil Rubenstein and **Flo Nakamura,** for use
of their photocopier and other assistance, and
Michael, for everything.

CONTENTS

Part 4: Family Relationships

Part 5: Mate Relationships

             Developing Intimacy 85
*Your intuition can help guide you to those with whom you
agreed to possibly mate. Honesty and communication are
keys to developing intimacy.*

Chapter 19   Working with Mate Relationships 106
*Opening to relationships without clinging to them allows
you to be balanced in them.*

                Room in Your Life 106
                Coming Close 106
                Asking the Universe 107
                An Abundance of Relationships 107
                Making Choices 107
                Marriage 108
                Flexibility 108
                Projection 109
                Fear 110
                Setting Boundaries 110
                Being Male 110
                A Light Touch.........................111
                Letting Go 112
                Balance...............................112
                Ending a Relationship.................113
                Healing the Rip 114
                Complementarity 114
                Pioneering 114

Chapter 20   Sexuality 116
Sex is a joining of energies. It can take many forms.

                Sex and Balance 116
                Eros and Agape 116
                Higher Intimacy First 117

Part 6: Communion

PREFACE

In our growth and healing as human beings, our core issues usually involve love: being loved by others, loving others, and finally, loving ourselves. Today we often explore our relationships with our parents, what our parents were and were not able to give us of love, and the effect that had on us. Some of us investigate issues around love from past lives. That is all very important work.

This book goes to an even more basic level: exploring the nature of love itself—what is love, and what is it to love and be loved? Seeing ourselves as *being* love, which is perhaps the ultimate perspective on love, puts our inner work in a different light. It doesn't eliminate the necessity of doing the work, but it does make it easier.

I have had some mistrust of the word *love*; perhaps you have as well. It is often associated with behavior that seems, well, unloving. The bickering and even violence often found in romantic relationships, and the hurts inflicted by adults on children in the name of love, are prime examples. It is useful to recognize that love and truth cannot be separated. What is not truthful is not loving, and vice versa. Defining *love* this way makes it clear that the word is often misused. We human beings do not yet really know all that much about love's reality.

Working with the material in this book, however, has given me more acceptance for our human condition, for the fact that we are still quite early in our process of learning love, this primary lesson of life. If we could do better, we would—this seems the most loving of attitudes.

I accessed the material in this book through a process called "channeling," working with a nonphysical entity referred to as "Michael." Before beginning reading the channeled material, you might find some background helpful.

MICHAEL CHANNELING

Channeling is a process of allowing a nonphysical intelligence to express through a person who is the "channel" or "channeler." It can be in words, energy, emotion, movement, and/or music, among other things. Michael is the name of a group or "entity" of 1,050 individual souls or "essences"[1] who have completed the physical and astral planes of creation, and teach from the causal plane. [*See the Glossary for definitions.*] This is why they refer to themselves as "we." They are not the same as the archangel Michael or other Michaels who are channeled. However, there are several other Michael books by other channels and authors who work with this same Michael.

Most of the other Michael books deal with the Michael teachings, which is a complex and fascinating body of information about the way we set up our lives. *The Journey of Your Soul—A Channel Explores Channeling and the Michael Teachings* is my contribution thus far to that body of information. *Loving from Your Soul*, like the other books in the Summerjoy Michael series,[2] does not attempt to cover the technical aspects of the Michael teachings in detail, although the teachings' principles pervade it. The few terms associated with the teachings are defined in the Glossary.

ORGANIZATION

More than half the material in this book is from lectures, most of which were given as part of the New York City "Michael Speaks" series. The rest of the material is from private sessions. Some of the chapters are compilations of passages from various lectures and private sessions. Most of those passages are in their own subchapter. If there are two or more passages

---

[1]Michael uses the word *essence* as a synonym for *soul* throughout this book.
[2]Upcoming titles in this series include *Growing Through Joy, Opening to Healing Energy,* and *Being in the World.* To be notified of their release, or to receive information about private sessions and workshops with the author, contact Summerjoy Press, 31423 S. Coast Hwy. #84, Laguna Beach, CA 97677-3056, 888-LIVE JOY (888-548-3569).

in a single subchapter, they are separated by double spacing. Questions are italicized and are also separated from Michael's responses by double spacing. Some chapters or entire sections contain material directed to specific people, yet have universal relevance. Unless implied by subtitles or questions, these are noted: *To a Specific Individual, To Specific Individuals,* or *Mostly to Specific Individuals.*

EDITING

I channel consciously. That means that I am awake and fully present during the process. Although the material does not originate with me, Michael makes use of the contents of my consciousness, and, to some degree, is limited by my limitations. (Transmitting information that is too foreign to a channel is difficult.) Although this material is well beyond what I could produce on my own, in a real sense it is mine, and I take full responsibility for it.

In general, I treated the original transcripts like first drafts, and polished them as I would my own writing, cutting, rearranging, and rewriting as necessary. Some passages needed little or no editing, while others required extensive revision. Most of the book's material was originally spoken, and what is clear orally may not be clear when it is transcribed, because speaking and writing are different media. Also, there was sometimes a need to translate from the personal to the universal, so that readers can relate. Lastly, some editing was necessary simply due to my imperfections as a channel and the difficulties inherent in extemporaneously translating complex concepts from the invisible to the visible. However, before publication I "brought in" Michael to get their modifications and "stamp of approval."

Using "s/he," "he or she," or alternating "he" and "she" all seemed awkward, so I decided to stick with just "he." *The Elements of Style* states that over time, "'he' has lost all suggestion of maleness in these circumstances." I hope that no one is offended by this choice.

This book does not contain Michael's comprehensive thoughts on any subject. I simply used the material I had, which came forth in response to specific individuals and groups.

Loving from Your Soul presupposes we each are a soul who has lived other lives, but believing in reincarnation, or even in channeling, is not necessary for an enjoyable and profitable reading of it. You can validate most of the ideas in it for yourself, and Michael encourages you to do so.

Interchanges with Michael are magical: full of healing, clarification, and upliftment. May you experience this magic as you read their words.

Shepherd Hoodwin
New York City
November, 1994

INTRODUCTION

We are all expanding and deepening our knowledge of love. Love is the primary force of the cosmos. As we learn greater love, we further our movement toward the great goal, agape,[3] which is the ability to love fully and unconditionally. In our relationships there is great opportunity to open ourselves to love.

The soul is an expression of the Tao, which is the source of love. By loving from your soul, you are loving truly. By loving truly, you are letting the Tao come clearly into your relationships so that they are transformed and contribute to the unfoldment of love's journey through the cosmos. This is the great purpose of existence.

This book is a collection of explorations on this subject. We hope that you find it both practically useful and spiritually illuminating.

Michael

---

[3]*Agape* is a Greek word pronounced *ah*-guh-pay or uh-*gah*-pay.

Part 1

THE NATURE
OF LOVE

Chapter 1

LOVE

We are a causal plane entity consisting of 1050 souls who have completed the physical plane cycle on earth. We speak to you not as outsiders but as ones who have experienced and in certain respects continue to experience what you are now dealing with in your life. We are playing the role of teacher, but that is merely something we are doing for the time being. We teach not because we are exalted or perfect, but because we learn in this way, just as you learn by hearing what we have to say and accepting it or rejecting it, as you choose. We may already be friends with you, even if you do not remember. If we are not yet friends, we view you as a future friend, so we greet you in that vein.

We are all here to do something together. Your truth is as precious to the universe as ours. Your wisdom has been gained by much experience, just as ours has. Your struggles and growth have enhanced the knowledge and well-being of all. You are significant. You are a part of the All, not like a drop of water that melts into the ocean, but like a cell in a vast body that creatively and individually adds to what is known by the entire organism. You are a conductor of the highest force of the universe, which is sometimes referred to by the name "love." You are a loving being. You came to this planet in a great act of love, as did we. Everything you have done, you have done out of love. Those who apparently do evil do it ultimately out of love, even if their actions are misguided for the moment.

You may think of yourself as a failure at love. Even if all your relationships have ended poorly, in your view, this is not the true measure of love. You undertook them with an expectation, at least unconsciously, that you would increase your knowledge of love, and in fact, you did. You may not have recognized all their lessons yet, but you will, at least on some level.

You do not make the same mistake twice; each mistake is always at least a little different. In any case, mistakes are not failures, in the sense that they should not have occurred. Had you been capable of doing otherwise, you would have. You lacked the true insight that would have allowed you to avoid making them. But no matter what you lack, you are perfect. Everything is in a state of becoming more than it is; otherwise, we would all be bored. Your lacks are opportunities for expansion.

When you leave the physical plane at the end of your life, you usually review it. No longer enmeshed in its intensity, you can more easily see clearly what you learned, and find love and compassion for yourself. You can better appreciate the worth of your experiences, both how much you gained and how much you helped others gain. You can even laugh about some of the things you took quite seriously during your life.

Children tend to be proud of their physical growth and development, and they do not have to do anything except live, mostly playing, for growth to occur. Unfortunately, in your culture, many children do not get to play as much as they would like; nevertheless, they play their way to growth. Adults can learn from this. We are not suggesting that you should party your life away and refuse to look at its issues, or that the way is always easy or clear. But growth can be fun and adventurous, and eventually leads to more life energy and greater well-being.

Ultimately, every step forward increases love. You are love, so every step you take forward increases what you are for the benefit of all. You cannot grow without increasing your ability to love, and you cannot love without growing. It is not selfish to pay attention to your own growth, because it gives you more to bring to others. The only thing that is selfish is what hurts others. That will inevitably hurt you also, because you are connected to everyone else by reason of being part of the same whole.

You may ask, "What do I do with my anger and hate?" Love them. At their heart, they are love designed to change or

keep out what does not belong, and this can increase love.
There is a place for anger and hate in the universe; otherwise
they would not exist. They are not destructive unless expressed
in a way that violates others' domain. Properly, they are directed at people's actions rather than at their being. If you do
express them destructively, learn from your experience and
forgive yourself. All experiences can contribute to your
growth.

Love your feelings. As you welcome them, your load
lightens. The first step of love is acceptance. Accept every part
of yourself as good. How many tapes do you have running
through your mind that say "bad boy" or "bad girl"? You are
not bad for anything you have done, and neither is anyone else.
This is the awareness love brings to a situation. You may
choose not to allow others to behave in certain ways in your
space—that is a different matter. But in love, you accept their
right to experience what they must experience to learn.

Every action has a reason for being. Hurtful actions are
often the enactment of internal conflicts on the stage of the
outer world. When people no longer need to act out their conflicts, they stop. When you love yourself fully, you stop
playing either aggressor or victim roles, partly because you are
not treating yourself in a violent, arbitrary, or unaccepting way,
or seeing yourself as powerless. Love is true power. Love is the
ultimate solution to all problems. ☜

Chapter 2

LOVE AND ANGER

Sometimes people think of hugs, gifts, and perhaps sex as being indicative of love. Sometimes they are, sometimes not. Love manifests in many forms, but love is not primarily defined by the form it takes. Love relates more to intent. The purer the intent, the more accurate the expression of love. If you would learn greater purity of love, be aware of your intent. Ultimately, the highest intent, and therefore the highest love, is the desire, the will, that the greatest good for all be served. (This does not, by the way, exclude your own good.)

What, then, of feelings that are not aligned with this intent? Perhaps you would like to strangle a coworker for something he did, or scream at the top of your lungs if one more salesman calls you on the phone, especially during dinner. Perhaps you are annoyed at your child because he keeps interrupting you. Do you stuff down your feelings and smile sweetly because, after all, you are a loving person and, therefore, you are not supposed to be feeling this way?

Everything in you has purpose. There is no dark place either within or outside you that is not ultimately good. All the forces moving in you are seeking to impel you to act creatively and perhaps forcefully. If they are ignored, they become stronger and stronger until they are finally acknowledged and appropriately acted upon. If it comes to the point where you are at wit's end, as in the examples we just gave, you have probably denied for a long time your impulse to act creatively. If you explode in anger, you may feel better for the moment, because some of the pressure is relieved, but your anger will likely return if you do not take creative action to address the reason for your anger.

Let's look at the example of the salesman calling you. The irritation you feel is an impulse to take creative action to protect your quietude. You might do this by using an answering machine. If your child is constantly interrupting you, perhaps he is telling you that he does not have challenges that stimulate him, and new art supplies or a football are in order. Maybe he is bothered by something he is not speaking about, and you could find out what that is. Perhaps you are not clearly communicating your love to him, and taking special time just for him would solve the problem.

Flying off the handle is usually not helpful or loving, but neither is repressing your emotions. That is not loving to yourself, for one thing. If you repress your emotions, you have to carry them with you, and you become heavy. Let your intent be that the highest good for all be served, and you will increasingly discover ways to manifest it.

What is the origin of love? Why was it introduced?

Love was created by the Tao as the primary expression of itself, as a way to feel itself, to know that it exists. It is something like stretching your legs when you wake up in the morning, partly so you know that they are there.

Love is the thread running through all existence. We all came from the Tao to expand love, to expand the Tao's awareness of itself, and love leads us back to the Tao. We take this expanded awareness back with us.

Why is it that in human life, love seems to come with things such as jealousy, egotism, and selfishness?

Love is all there is. It is either experienced in a pure way, or it is distorted by fear. These are fear-based distortions of love in human relationships, manifestations of immaturity.

Love is the chief lesson, the lesson behind every other lesson. When you are first learning something, you are usually not very good at it. The physical plane is the primary school of love, and most people are not yet very skilled at it. Those of us who have been through this school understand how difficult its lessons can be. ᏨᏍᎧ

LEARNING LOVE

A n artist can learn something from every work of art he creates. Each work of art expands art, because it is unique. Whether it is deemed good or bad, it is still a new, never-before-created effort. Therefore, new ground has been broken and art has been advanced, at least to some small degree. Some works are imitative, while others are more original, yet even what is imitative has something new in it. Few artists are great, but every artist progresses if he applies himself. Each lifetime builds on the one before, and artistic skill can grow from lifetime to lifetime. Eventually, every soul who chooses to invest the necessary effort can achieve a high level of artistry. If a child demonstrates native ability for art, no doubt he had previous lives that brought this talent into being. Each great artist was once an average artist, and before that, unskilled, in previous lifetimes. Art is an essential part of the lessons of this planet. While most souls do not aspire to a high level of artistic achievement, virtually everyone wants to take advantage of the opportunity to experience artistry, and therefore has at least one lifetime in which there is some artistic study. It is like going to New York and making certain not to miss the opportunity to see the Statue of Liberty.

Whatever you are specifically studying, you have come to learn love. Every experience on earth is a lesson in love and in some way expands love, the mistakes as well as the successes. Even a great artist makes many mistakes. It is as important for the artist to know what does not work as to know what does. The more original the artist, the more mistakes he makes, because by definition, originality takes you into uncharted territory. There is no body of knowledge to guide you. Every lifetime, to some degree, takes you through uncharted territory. Some people live relatively conservatively and seek the familiar, but even so, they cannot escape some surprises. Others are more adventurous and their lives are full of new experiences. If those who pioneer are sometimes awkward or less than completely successful, those who come later can achieve greater success based on their work. Generally, the first to experiment with new forms in art or music do not bring forth the ultimate expressions of those forms. Nevertheless, without the pioneers, those ultimate expressions would have no chance of being created.

If you are on a spiritual path, you are likely to be on the leading edge in discovering new, higher forms of love. Others may think that you are a little weird. What is new is generally uncomfortable. Your efforts will not always be unqualified successes. Fortunately, you are not attempting to develop these forms alone—you have all those who are fellow pioneers. There are those who will try to convince you that the world is flat and that you are going to sail off the edge. For all you know for certain, they may be right, but you sail on anyway. This is the spirit of the explorer.

In the development of new art forms, trends come and go, but each contributes to the overall progression. Likewise, there are many new age techniques that aid the study of love but will eventually not be needed. It is important to maintain an awareness of the overall lesson—love. The point is not technique. Techniques are necessary, but they are means to an end; they are not ends in themselves. If you wish to appraise the value of a technique for yourself, ask, "Is this in some way expanding my capacity for love?" If it is, then at least for the moment, it is worthwhile for you. When it ceases to aid you in expanding love, it is wise to leave it behind.

Channeling is a technique. It is a means, not an end. Channeling has no intrinsic value on its own, just as a telephone has no intrinsic value on its own. It is the communication over the telephone or through the channel that can give it value. If our penetration through this channel aids in magnifying the experience of love, it is worthwhile. This is the purpose of all true teachings.

Love is all-inclusive. It cannot be limited to narrow aspects of itself. Love is not just soft and nurturing. It is also strong and penetrating. Love is the force that increases the integrity of the universe. Whatever is required to do this is loving.

Integrity is related to functionality. When something contributes to a higher level of functionality, it is loving. For example, it can be a loving act to dismantle an engine that is not working properly, that lacks integrity. Then it can be rebuilt, or the parts that are still in good working order can be used in other engines.

Likewise, it can be a loving act to dismantle a relationship that is not working properly, that lacks integrity. A relationship has integrity if in it, you are more effective in contributing to the well-being of yourself and others than you are outside it. If a relationship impedes well-being, it does not have integrity and will tend to break down. But even that is not antithetical to the purposes of love, because some good spare parts may come out of it, or perhaps it can be rebuilt.

A time comes with any machine when it is worn out and not worth repairing any more. For one machine, that might be soon after being manufactured. For another, that might be a hundred years later. It depends partly on who has been using it. Relationships, being alive, can be regenerated, but they do not stay in the same form forever, because you are growing and changing. It is important to be able to discern when the form of a relationship of any kind has outlived its usefulness. Sometimes the greatest contribution to the magnification of love is achieved alone, and sometimes it is achieved in partnership with another or with many others. This can change over time. However, you can learn something from every relationship, and every relationship expands love to some degree.

Love achieves whatever is of the greatest benefit. It may first flush out what needs to be eliminated, which can be uncomfortable, but ultimately, love brings increased well-being to all concerned.

MEDITATION

Close your eyes and feel your body. Your body is not just your flesh. Feel it as far out as it extends from your skin. Ask that your body receive love. Ask that this love bring balance, alignment, and attunement with the source of love, the Tao. 🍵

Chapter 4

EXPANDING LOVE

Love is an ever-present reality. It does not have to be caused to exist. However, it can be expanded. Each of us is an example of love seeking to experience new aspects of itself. Love would become bored after a while being the "same old" infinite reality. It wants to increase, so you, an individual spark within the eternal fire, continually set out to see what happens when you plant yourself in new situations, asking "How does love handle this?"

When a problem is solved, love has expanded. There are problems everyone is seeking to solve because they relate to the experiments that love is undertaking through all humanity. These include "How can I get along with my fellows and honor myself at the same time?" and "How can the male side of things be different from yet in union with the female side of things, both externally and internally?" There are also your personal problems that are your individual experiments in love.

The complete solution to a problem is not merely intellectual. It involves all levels of being, including its physical, emotional, and spiritual aspects, because love encompasses all levels of being. If you come up with an intellectual idea that might be helpful in solving a problem, you still have to implement it physically, and that may require emotional and spiritual changes. If it is to be successful, the solution must provide an expansion of love.

Love is the power behind and beyond all others. One who has the greatest quantity and quality of love has the most true power. It may not appear this way. Your employer may have a lot of power insofar as your life is concerned, but not a great deal of love. Dictators may be politically all-powerful in their countries. On the surface, they have power, but their power has no fundamental effect on your internal state unless you allow it to.

There is a perception that those who are loving are milquetoasts—in other words, they have little power. People point out that Jesus was apparently powerless to prevent his crucifixion, which seems to prove that when compared to the strength of political systems, love is a minor force. Let us examine this a little more carefully.

Suppose that you are the most politically and financially powerful person on earth, and you are dying of a disease. You go to the greatest doctors, but they cannot help you. Then you have the good fortune to meet someone like Jesus. He lays his hands upon you and heals you. Who has more power?

We are not saying that being a healer per se is a more important profession or a higher calling than being a financier or politician; Jesus would have been equally powerful and effective as a politician had that been his task. How could he heal other people? Where did he get this power? Healing comes from love—love is the healing power. Jesus could heal because of the quantity and quality of love he had.

External power cannot bring contentment or well-being. This does not deny that those with the ability to be effective in the outer world are often gratified by that. But if you do not have well-being, all the effectiveness in the world is for naught. On the other hand, if you do have some well-being without basic life skills, it is likely to be challenged constantly; both are necessary, but well-being springs from love rather than from external effectiveness.

True power has influence, but it is not fundamentally power over others. Jesus obviously had great influence. His presence changed the world, yet he was not trying to change the world. He was not trying to become a king, for example. He could have—he had quite a following. Had he desired, he might have overthrown the reigning government. He might have even built an empire. He was young, charismatic, pretty well educated, and savvy. There would have been nothing wrong with him doing that had that been his path. But even without putting forth effort in this regard, he had enormous impact. Had he wished to, he probably could have avoided the crucifixion. However, he was so powerful that he did not need to.

The greater your inner mastery, the less you desire to master others or control what is outside you. The greater your love, the greater your ability to simply exist and to have the mere fact of existence be its own reward. Then, out of that existence, you may do much. Jesus was a busy man, doing healings, among other things, but we doubt that he lived for his healing practice. We doubt that he said, "I healed twelve people today. That is so satisfying. It makes me want to go on and try to heal fourteen people tomorrow." It did not really matter. He was already satisfied being himself. The doing was a pleasure because it came from being. Some activities may have been more pleasurable than others for him, but we doubt that he lived for the pleasurable ones.

We are not making a pitch for Christianity. There have been many people who were great in their capacity to love. It was those with lesser capacity who formed schools of thought around them. The point of this exploration is to underline your own capacity to love.

Any skill you practice grows in its breadth and depth. If you wish to be able to love more, you need to practice love. How can you do this? For one thing, simply be aware of love in your life. When you see a loving action, acknowledge it, whether it is your own or someone else's. When you are less than loving, acknowledge that, too, and ask yourself how you might have been loving in that situation.

We are not speaking merely of behaviors, but of a quality. Those who devote their lives to doing good deeds are not necessarily loving. When actions spring from love, they feel true, right on the mark. It is like looking at a slide that is exactly in focus. A slide of mountains may be quite beautiful, but if it is shown out of focus, it hurts your eyes to look at it. Only when the slide is in focus can you relax while looking at it and melt into the beauty of the scene before you. Truly loving actions are like a slide projecting through a lens that is focused.

Our greatest concern when being channeled is not the correctness of word choices, but the love transmitted. The potential for that is based not just on the channel's capacity but on the capacity of those listening, because we cannot give more than can be received; there would be no point. We work to establish an atmosphere that supports full openness to love. When you love to the maximum of your capacity, your capacity grows.

The universe is concerned with expanding love, not only in experiencing greater quantities and qualities of love, but in experiencing love in new ways. This is fundamentally what the game is about. This is why the universe exists. We encourage growth, which is ultimately growth in the capacity to love, for this reason.

Love is the greatest wealth available. It is the course of wisdom to value wealth. Physical wealth is a small symbol of true wealth. There is not necessarily anything wrong with having physical wealth, but why settle for merely the symbol when you can have the real thing?

Love is not in denial of anything, because love is connected to all things. Love is the outpouring of the Tao, the All, and includes all things. It includes and sees beyond all confusion, pain, so-called negative feelings, and positive ones, too. They are all acceptable to love.

When you know love, your difficulties do not disappear overnight. However, you see them in a new way and find higher levels of effectiveness in dealing with them. The saying that love is the answer is true, but it does not refer merely to being romantically in love, although that is a wonderful thing. Since you are love, you are the answer.

In learning what love is, you are learning who you are. In expanding love, you are expanding who you are. You are here to do that.

It looks like the universe is process- rather than goal-oriented.

The universe is interested in both the achievement of goals and the experience of process. Goals are achieved through process, so they are not separate. The earth is the result of some of the universe's goals. The universal consciousness did not just throw together some substances totally experimentally without regard to what might happen, saying, "Oh, that's nice," when earth happened to result.

The universe is half female energy, which is process-oriented, and half male energy, which is goal-oriented. The process brings about the goals, but the goals are flexible. They are fine-tuned as they are approached, based on what is learned in the process leading to them. Goals and process work together, process leading to goals, and goals leading to more process.

Everyone, at his core, is love; behind love is the Tao. The Tao is the undimensional All, the ground of being. The Tao creates the dimensional universe in which we live. The universe has seven planes of existence [*see Glossary*]:[4] physical, astral, causal, akashic, mental, messianic, and buddhaic. Each plane is at a faster, or higher, rate of vibration than the one before it. You fragment from the Tao and are returning to oneness with it. Along the way, you pass through each of these planes. Returning to complete union with the Tao is the goal, but the process along the way is equally important. It is not like being in a race whose only purpose is the trophy. It is more like taking a vacation, going around the world.

Suppose you start in New York and you want to end up back in New York. The goal, in the sense of your final destination, is New York. However, you do not rush through London, Paris, Istanbul, and Tokyo just so you can get back to New York as quickly as possible. The whole vacation is valuable and valid. In the same way, you are moving toward the destination that is also where you began: union with the Tao. You

---

[4]For more information about the planes of existence, and other elements of Michael's technical teachings, see the author's *The Journey of Your Soul— A Channel Explores Channeling and the Michael Teachings*.

bring back to it all you experienced on the way—that is your contribution to the expansion of love.

We are of the causal plane. We look forward to our movement into the higher planes. This will come naturally as we do what we are doing here. The same is true for you.

How do joy, contentment, and thankfulness relate to love?

Love is the primary vibration. Joy fills one who is acting in love. That filling brings fulfillment or contentment.

Thankfulness opens the door to love. Thankfulness includes, rather than denies. It is an acknowledgment of what is and a statement, which is the statement of love, that what is, is okay. Thankfulness is also the starting point of change, because change begins from what is. Thankfulness releases all things into the whole.

When I surrender to love, I then have an emotional reaction denying it. How can I avoid this?

It is not that you are generating denial of love. It is that you are allowing already-present denial to come to the surface. This is positive. Heretofore, you had been denying your denial of love. Loving and accepting it gives you a chance to release it. Guilt, not love, judges and condemns what is unloving. Love what is unloving in you, and also your guilt about it and judgment of it.

How can we know that what we think of as love is in fact that elemental source from which all life comes?

Love has a quality you can learn to discern. It "feels right." It is truthful and inclusive. There is no objective measurement to confirm that you are experiencing love. You can only trust your intuition and do your best. If you do, your capacity to discern love will grow. We are all learning this skill.

How can you maintain loving feelings when dealing with diffi-cult people or circumstances?

If you are reacting unproductively, disengage, step back or at least slow down, and think about what is coming up in you and how you can be more loving and appropriate in your expression. If, over time, you work through what tends to interrupt your conscious experience of love, you will have fewer and fewer interruptions.

Rather than attacking others, simply communicate without judgment what you are feeling or the needs you are perceiving. Love does not make others wrong. It does not make yourself wrong either. In love, you may state facts you need to state; you also respect facts that are real for others. If you find your-self either attacking others or trying to be loving by repressing your feelings, you have not yet accurately perceived love.

People sometimes go from one extreme to another. They stuff down their feelings for a while; then they explode. Nei-ther extreme feels good. Love is in the middle, where there is no need for repression or inappropriate expression. Instead, your expression is thoughtful and well-timed.

You mentioned that the universe seeks to find new ways to love. Could you say more about that?

Everything new offers a new way to love. In this era there is much technological creativity providing many new ways to love. For example, the universe is now experiencing love through human beings talking on telephones and performing for television broadcasts. These are slightly different experi-ences than their nontechnological counterparts, offering new choices. That is not fundamentally different than nature creat-ing a new kind of flower, which also offers love a new avenue of expression.

However, the form itself does not have to be new. You are constantly creating in your life. You might create artistically through art, music, poetry, novels, or other types of literature.

You might create a home, or food or clothing within that home. Almost everyone creates conversations each day. There are also inner creations: atmosphere, emotions, and thoughts, for instance. Lives are full of creation. We are all creators. The choices you make when you create move from what was created before into something new, something that has not been known.

For example, composers, of necessity, build on what went before. Some use the musical forms of the past. Others create new forms or styles that relate to what came before but go beyond it. Compositions using forms or styles from the past may bring something new into them. Compositions using both new content and new forms or styles take newness further.

If you are a secretary, for instance, there might be appropriate limits to your creativity. If you are too creative, you might incur the displeasure of your employer. Yet you are still making choices as to how you type and edit a letter, how you sit while you are typing, how you interact with the other people in your office, and so on. Any choice that springs from love expands love.

Everything you do is from love to at least some extent, because everything is ultimately part of love. However, there are portions of love that are less aware than others that they are love. The more you are aware that you are love, and the more creative you are in the expression of it, the more you expand love. ❦

Part 2

RELATIONSHIP
WITH YOURSELF

Chapter 5

LOVING YOURSELF

There is much new awareness that it is necessary to love yourself in order to love others. What is the nature of loving yourself? There are many different ways of seeing this: treating yourself as you would treat someone you highly respect and admire; giving yourself time for things that matter most to you; eating your food with affection, so that the love you give the food then goes into your body; and so forth.

Loving yourself, however, goes beyond such things. Loving is a unified experience that does not cut off any portion of your reality. When you are loving yourself, you are loving others. When you are loving others, you are loving yourself. When you are having joy in what you are doing, you are giving joy to the world—there is no separation between you and the world. If you have been holding back from treating yourself well for fear that doing so would detract from more important things, you are not seeing the connection between what you do for yourself and your contribution to the rest of what is. When you caress yourself, you are immediately giving the planet a warm and vitalizing touch; you are the planet. When you shout with glee, you release a ripple of color that the stars witness with a sense of gladness; you are the stars, the witness to your own joy. When you truly love yourself or love in any way, you leave a faint but unmistakable aroma of magic in your wake. Is this not at least as great a contribution to humanity as accomplishing item number ten on your "to do" list?

Any act of love is a step in the evolution of life. Love does not differentiate between the love you give yourself and the love you give others. Loving yourself is not self-centered. If you truly love yourself, your actions do not exclude others' well-being. Your true self-interest includes what is best for everyone. If you do what you truly love to do, you are in harmony with the whole.

Love is. You cannot honor the wisdom of the ages without coming to love. You cannot love others without loving yourself. You cannot love yourself without loving others. You cannot express love without being love. You are love, so that is not a problem.

"What about the parts of me that do not feel loving?" you may ask. "What about my anger toward my boss, my mate, or my neighbors?" The answer is simple: Love your anger. Love those who have perhaps trespassed against you, and love the force in you that seeks to protect you from further trespass or to impel you to appropriate action. Love it all.

Loving yourself has vast ramifications. It is not simply a way to increase your effectiveness and enjoyment; it is your primary means of coming to know the force that activates the universe. ✸

Chapter 6

BEAUTY, COMPARISON, AND CHOICE

It was not that long ago that only the wealthy could afford enough food to become large, so being large was considered beautiful; being thin was considered "bony" and unattractive. Throughout much of the same period, many people worked outdoors in the fields; their skin became tanned and weathered. The well-to-do could stay indoors and therefore not be suntanned, so being untanned was also considered beautiful. Of course, that is reversed now, since most people work indoors, although the pendulum is swinging back, with the current concern about skin cancer.

True physical beauty is not a function of conforming to the current fashion. It is largely a result of health, grooming (which includes choice of color, style, and cut in your clothing), and, not insignificantly, how much you are allowing your true inner self to come forth.

The more a person believes that she is beautiful, the more that actual beauty will be impressed upon others. That belief can become so strong that others' beliefs about large and thin bodies, for instance, can be suspended in her presence. She might still choose to reduce (or increase) her weight, but not because it will make her beautiful, since she already is.

Behind beliefs about large and thin bodies, there is an even more fundamental one to examine—the belief in comparison. Most people are taught to compare at a very early age, but it becomes especially pronounced in school. Only so many people can get A's, and it is usually based on comparison rather than on any absolute scale. If you were in a "smarter" class, the competition was more fierce for those A's. You might have been made to feel that your worth depended on them. If you got better grades, you were considered better than others. However, the idea that someone can be better or worse is a fallacy. The truth is that everyone *is* a winner; everyone is ultimately the winner of his own game, the game of choice.

You are here to make choices. You choose day by day, and you live with your choices, learning to make them more skillfully. Your past choices that created your present body weight, job, and relationships were "moves" you made in your game. All of them helped you improve your game, and continue to do so. No one has the right to tell you that you made bad choices—you made the choices you made. They were neither good nor bad; they were the best ones you knew how to make at the time, and the choices you are making now are the best ones you know how to make now. If you had complete "enlightenment," you wouldn't need this game at all. You would be playing another game.

The main reason one might wish to have made "better" choices is to win the comparison game. Ultimately, you can never win that game. You can be seemingly better than everyone else in one way or even in many ways, but still feel that you are losing the game in some other way. Then that way is likely to become all-important to you.

The comparison game is not the game you are here to play. It is preferable to play the game of choice, which is more fun, because there are no losers. If you make a choice that has consequences you later find that you do not like, you can make a different choice next time—that is how you learn. Even the best chess players make moves that end up trapping them, but the point is always the next move. ☟

✳ Chapter 7 ✳

NEW BELIEFS ABOUT THE WORLD
To Someone Lonely

Y ou are a beautiful soul. There is nothing undeserving in who you are. If you can see your present circumstance as being nothing more than an unfinished canvas upon which you are learning to paint your vision, you will have a better platform from which to act. If, on the other hand, you become too identified with the lacks you see in your life, interpreting them as indications of something wrong with you or with the world, it will be harder for you to create your vision.

Things are not as dark as they sometimes look when you are purging old "stuff." What you are purging tends to crowd out an awareness of what is good in your life. You might list everything good you can think of and just acknowledge it. We are not suggesting that you gloss over what you are not satisfied with, but it is important to see clearly where you are. If you are painting a picture, it is important to see what you have on the canvas, looking at what you want to keep as well as what is not yet finished.

You create your reality from your beliefs. The belief that you are alone in the world may have been formed during a lifetime when you literally were alone. Now you continue to create that reality. The situation has changed, but your belief has not. During times of purging, old beliefs are brought to bear more intensely than usual so that they can be seen and released. That is why you are feeling the loneliness more acutely. It is important to release the belief that you are alone and have to be, so that your experience can change.

Also, being alone or an outsider can be a form of self-protection. Although it does not feel good, you may believe that it feels better than being part of something you do not like or that you feel may bring harm to you. So you can also examine this belief.

How do you feel about the world? Part of you no doubt longs to be an "insider," but listen for the part of you that does not. Many people have such conflicting feelings. When part of you wants to go east and part of you wants to go west, you do not move much. There is not yet in your being a unity of purpose.

You can find out why part of you wants to remain an outsider. The key, ultimately, to the healing you seek is changing not only how you feel about yourself but how you see yourself. It is not just a matter of learning to love and accept yourself, although that is very important. It is a matter of your self-image coming clear. You need to recognize your present image if you are going to make it more accurate. Your total self-image is your most important creation for yourself.

It helps to recognize that you are not as different from others as you may have thought. If you get beyond the surface, even the people you most envy have many of the same feelings and issues you do. There are unique factors for everyone, but not many people are completely satisfied with themselves or their lives. Those who have what for you seem like the answers often feel that something else is the answer for them. This is not to discourage you from increasing your abundance in any way. We simply wish to give you a greater sense that there are many potential allies who can support you in your quest, just as you can support them.

It is almost impossible to live on the physical plane without some hurt. You experience the hurt more intensely than you might, so it seems life-threatening. This is because of other hurts that have not healed. New hurts trigger memories of the old. For example, if you were in a relationship and your partner chose to end it, you would not only experience the natural hurt of ending a relationship; all similar unhealed hurts would also come up. These might include, for example, the feeling of abandonment when your father left your family, in this lifetime or in another. If you recognize that you are carrying hurts from the past, you can deal with them separately. You can be more objective about your present hurt, and realize that you can handle it.

Healing has two aspects. It is like having surgery: first, the old diseased tissue is removed; then the healthy tissue that was around it grows in, and the system stabilizes itself. Catharsis is the equivalent of removing diseased tissue.

If you had trauma in your childhood, you were probably not able to process a lot of it at the time. However, as an adult, you can, as you allow your "child within" to tell his story. No doubt you held back many tears because there was no one there to hear them. Perhaps you had to pull yourself up by your bootstraps and focus on surviving. Instead of allowing your feelings to move so that they could heal, they got stuck and became like diseased tissue. Now, at this later date, you can move them through.

This can be done without full recall of the circumstances. You need to access the feelings themselves, although remembering the circumstances may help you access the feelings. It is hard to do deep healing work like this completely on your own, just as you would probably not want to perform surgery on yourself even if you were a doctor. So you might want to work with a counselor you trust as you begin to release your old feelings.

Then, to let the healthy tissue fill in, so to speak, provide yourself with a nurturing atmosphere where a healthy view of life can grow. Just recognizing that your beliefs are not necessarily complete allows you to begin to act on different beliefs. For example, take at least a tentative attitude that the world is full of potential friends, and begin to act on that belief, so that you invite people to be in your life. If you can also take the tentative attitude that the world wants you to succeed and is generous, you can begin to act on that as well. Once you have experiences that back up these new beliefs, it will be easier for you to maintain them, especially as you are recognizing and releasing your old ones. ❦

ᘏᕽᐣ Chapter 8 ᑫᕽᐤ

LONELINESS

Every soul originates in total union with the Tao and is being drawn back to it. The youngest soul, having come from the Tao not that long ago, remembers this union. After a while, it is forgotten for a time so that lessons of individuality can be emphasized, but the magnetic pull toward it remains. Physical sex is an expression through the body of this magnetic pull.

Usually the impulse toward oneness is personalized. When people fall in love with a specific person, they are selecting someone with whom to practice oneness. It is not necessary to limit such practice to sexual partners. Another way to practice is by blending spiritual energies in a group. If sex is defined in its broadest sense as being a blending of energies, it is conceivable that you could experience a rich and varied sex life twenty-four hours a day, blending energies with everything in your life in whatever way is appropriate. It is the nature of energy to seek blending. Through blending, it expands and ascends.

One of the saddest emotions in humanity is loneliness. Loneliness is the lack of the experience of blending energies, because opportunities to do so are not discerned or taken advantage of. It is easier to blend energies when there is another person available with whom you wish to do so. Nonetheless, it is possible to be alone and still blend energies. You can commune with nature: animals, plants, minerals, the earth itself, the wind, the stars, the sun, and the moon. You can commune with nonphysical beings: loved ones who are astral, or teachers who are causal or on other planes. You can commune with great souls through the art they created, including music, paintings, and literature. You can commune with friends who are physical but not present, through your heart. You can allow an internal blending of energies between your conscious mind and other aspects of yourself, such as your "child within," past-life selves, and especially, your essence.[5]

Taking responsibility for having the highest experience available to you in all you do allows you to have a fulfilling life. If you are standing in line at the grocery store, you can at least blend energies within. You can perhaps blend with the checker by being in the present moment and sensing what kind of connection could be made in spirit, either in your own consciousness only or through a gesture, a smile, or a word. When you drive, you can blend with your car. You can blend energies with your food as you prepare it, if you do, and as you eat it. You can take responsibility for blending with others in any group situation in which you find yourself, not losing your own boundaries, but letting energy move. That is what energy naturally does.

You can only blend energies if you are present. If you are spacing out, your mind rattling on about something else, you will not be blending energies effectively, even with your own mind. If you come into the present moment and blend with your mind when it has pressing concerns, you can better see those concerns and what can be done about them, offering healing and insight.

Being alone is an opportunity to practice blending. If you are looking for a mate and undertake such practice, you will be more capable of blending skillfully when you have one. Also, because of your increased abilities, you are more likely to attract a mate with a larger and more sensitive ability to blend.

You probably know couples who have been together for a long time and still do not know each other very well, because they are not very skilled at blending. However, you cannot know someone else more than you know yourself. Someone who is asleep, unconscious of who he is, cannot be conscious of who someone else is.

----

[5]A reminder: Michael uses the word *essence* as a synonym for *soul* throughout this book.

You said that when you're in a checkout line, you can blend energies with the checker. I find that sometimes when I casually do that, it makes the other person uneasy. Usually I back away if someone is getting fidgety from my looking too closely at him.

You can sometimes share something with others without their being conscious of it. For example, you can see another person as being part of you and feel a connection with him, broadcasting your good wishes to him in your heart. When you do that, he may respond energetically.

There are many reasons someone might be uncomfortable consciously blending energies. He may misinterpret your friendliness as being a sexual overture. It could be that he is struggling with a problem and is not interested in coming out of that.

Unfortunately, many people are terrified of intimacy, which is what blending brings. It can look dangerous. They may be afraid of being hurt, or of being exposed, due to a deep sense of shame, or of not being deserving, because of a feeling of worthlessness.

When you run up against fear of intimacy in someone else, your offering of blending needs to be subtle and appropriate to his level and kind of openness. If you are insensitive to what he can receive, you will not have the positive effect you are seeking. For example, if you insist that your blending with others take the form of hugs, and you try to hug the supermarket checker, he will probably not accept your offering. Presumptions in such cases are usually self-serving. If you have to hug someone, it is probably because you want a hug rather than because you are really interested in the other person and what you can share. Knowing what you can share with another comes through practicing being sensitive to that.

When you blend in whatever ways are available to you, loneliness is minimized if not eliminated. ✇

Chapter 9

BEING AT YOUR SOURCE

Universal power is available, but is usually not accessed except in severely constricted ways by most on the physical plane. If it is accessed prematurely, it can be destructive. The ideas through which universal power manifests must be sound. When they are, the power benefits the whole. Therefore, it is useful to examine the ideas you hold through which you would have this power manifest.

Ideas about relationships are often crystallized quite early. Infants see their relationships primarily in terms of meeting personal needs, and this viewpoint tends to remain through adulthood. It is so pervasive that it is usually taken for granted. Yet this idea can be an obstacle to manifesting universal power in relationships. Relationships based on this idea in which some universal power is accessed tend to be destructive.

Manifesting universal power constructively is more challenging in a relationship than on your own, but is also potentially more powerful and rewarding. Those who experience more universal power on their own than in relationships may be limited by the idea that relationships are primarily for meeting their needs.

The less space in a relationship taken with meeting individual needs, the more there is space available for other things. Many people cannot imagine what could lie beyond meeting their individual needs, which indicates how seldom individual needs are truly met. There is nothing wrong with meeting individual needs; on the contrary, individual needs must be met to an adequate degree in order to manifest universal power. But if a relationship is predominantly about meeting individual needs, the manifestation of universal power in it is severely limited. We are not suggesting that you try to do everything yourself and pretend that your needs are being met when they are not. There is a balance here, and learning to accept support is important. But when you do what you can for yourself, there is more space in your relationship.

Meeting individual needs can be a by-product of manifesting universal power. For example, you can manifest universal power in your work. As a by-product, it provides you with income, which you need, but your focus is not on the income; it is on the larger accomplishment. Likewise, your relationships can provide love and nurturing as by-products. They do not have to be your focus if you are each already loving and nurturing yourself. You are free to concentrate on manifesting universal power.

Many people see meeting their needs in financial terms. People usually do not feel that they have enough money, so that becomes a focus. They may see their primary relationship as a means to reach financial security. Those who become wealthy and feel that they finally have enough money start to see meeting their needs in other terms.

The ultimate need is for love. An infant may cry for milk or to have its diapers changed; that is love to an infant. The person who seeks money does so because to him, that is love. Whatever seems to be your unmet needs represent love to you.

At your core, you are a spark of the Tao, which is not only your source, but the source of love. When you identify with your source, so that you no longer seek love but feel yourself to be part and parcel of it, you do not look to other people to be your source of love. This is one way of describing the paramount lesson of the physical plane. It is not easily gained, but just knowing that this lesson is the goal can help you reach it.

Being at your source means that nothing has to be a certain way for you to be contented; being at your source is contentment. Paradoxically, your power to create is multiplied, so you tend to manifest more of what you would enjoy having. An example is actors who are unattached to getting a particular part—they do not see that part as their source—and are therefore more likely to get it, because they are free to do their best work when they audition. Those who see the part as their source, necessary to their well-being, are likely to project their fear of not getting it, which can be off-putting. When you are at your source, your power can move. Looking toward an outside source that may or may not be reliable, such as a director who may or may not give an actor a part, reduces your experience of power.

Some people have babies to get love. Sometimes babies do not smile and coo adorably; they scream and cry. If you are meeting their needs, this will happen less than if you are not, but it does happen. If your baby is your source of love—if, for you, that relationship is primarily about meeting *your* needs— you may feel that you have lost that source when he cries and seems to reject you, when you cannot get him to smile at you. Likewise, sometimes your mate cannot be there for you. If you are invested in his meeting your needs, you may feel abandoned.

Universal power comes from your source; you must be there to access it. Every experience offers this important lesson. Fear generally results from people thinking that their needs must be met by outside sources, but that they might not be. Fear has a place—it is meant to be a warning to make you more alert in dangerous situations. But fear often stems from an absence of trust due to a lack of experience of being at the source. When you lose your fears that your needs will not be met, you are truly free. Even if, for instance, you are in the midst of a famine and starvation is a possibility, if you are at your source, you are in position to take full advantage of opportunities to generate or attract food. You are also able to live longer on less food if you are not burning energy being anxious. Even if death is the result, when you are at your source, you can meet it without fear. Your unmet needs do not control you, even though you do all you can to meet them.

We are not suggesting that you should put on a face that says "Everything is fine with me" when that is not the case. It is better to bring your fears into the open. There is nothing wrong with feeling fear; in acknowledging it, you can also acknowledge your source and open further to it, which can help dissipate your fear.

Also, we are not suggesting that you pretend that you have no unmet needs. Many people are ashamed of their unmet needs, so they hide them. Acknowledging your unmet needs is the first step in meeting them, but also in getting beyond them, whether or not they are immediately met. Getting beyond them is the beginning of freedom. Some couples who thought themselves unable to have a child conceive soon after adopting. The reason is that they stop looking for their need to give birth to be met—they get beyond it, in this case by filling it in another way. Therefore, their power can move. Perhaps they would have also conceived had they gotten beyond it by just letting it go.

Knowing that you are the most influential power in your life will help put you at your source. Many people feel that they are a victim of circumstances. Someone at his source knows that he is the primary creator of his circumstances, and that life is simply a matter of making choices.

Being at your source is the best support you can give others for being at theirs. However, it is not a matter of being hard, telling someone to just get beyond his unmet needs and be at his source. If he knew how to do that, he would probably do it. If you listen to someone speak about his unmet needs, you are not necessarily empowering those needs as excuses to not be at his source. It is important not to make the needs look more powerful than his source, but if you are at your source, your listening and helping him meet his needs can also help him be at his source. You can demonstrate how someone at his source lovingly handles his needs. This can be seen with children. Parents represent the source to their children; in effectively filling their children's needs, parents teach them how to be at their source. Some parents are afraid to spoil their children, and think that they might do so if they always come, for example, when their children cry. Although parents cannot always be there immediately, the more they fill their children's needs, the more their children will grow into a state of being able to fill their own needs.

Even when you are at your source, a need can persist un-met for some time. Working with someone else who is at his source, especially someone who does not have that particular unmet need, can accelerate progress toward meeting it. Taking responsibility for meeting your needs does not preclude seek-ing support and insight from others. In fact, that may be the most effective way of taking responsibility. Seeking support for meeting your needs is not the same as expecting others to meet them for you.

By definition, being at your source is taking responsibility. It is the most effective way to meet your needs. If a person needs a greater experience of love, and is primarily looking to others to give it to him, he now has two needs: the need for love, and the need for others to give it to him in the way he wishes. On that basis, he is likely to attract those who are also not at their source and who therefore increase his sense of need.

In a good relationship, each offers the other support for the work he is doing to meet his own needs, but ideally the rela-tionship is not primarily about meeting needs. You might say that it is about playing the game that you are here to play. The word "game" suggests enjoyment. If the game were just about meeting needs, it would be dreary. You might meet needs while playing, but the game is about the joy of playing.

Some people have greater needs and require more time to meet them than others. An appropriate balance for one person is not the same for another. You do what you need to do. But as you are effective in meeting your needs from your source, there is more room in your life for activities beyond them that are satisfying, productive, and joyful, allowing you to construc-tively manifest greater universal power.

Part 3

RELATIONSHIPS
IN THE WORLD

❧ Chapter 10 ❧

INNER AND OUTER DOORS OF THE HEART

Sometimes people take mind-expanding narcotics; this is occasionally productive, but usually not, because there is not commensurate expansion of the heart. There are no drugs for this. The heart opens when it feels safe and when there is something it can open to. Because their spiritual faculties are relatively shut down, most people have seen the opening of their hearts only in terms of other people. When people fail them, sometimes there is a substitute such as a beloved animal. However, everyone can learn to open his heart inwardly. This is an essential skill for those on the spiritual path.

The heart has two doors: inner and outer. Sometimes, when you open the outer door of your heart to something external, such as another person, your inner door opens as well, but if you do not learn to keep your inner door open, it will likely slam shut when you close your outer door. On the other hand, if you open your inner door first, your outer door can open and close as it is appropriate with no effect on the inner door.

One way to learn to keep your inner door open is to feel it fully when it is open and imprint that feeling vividly in your consciousness. Let the intensity of that moment grow. Close your eyes, perhaps, and let it envelop you. Ask yourself to learn to let that experience come more and more. You might assign it a tangible symbol, such as the sun, an ocean wave, a cloud, or something else you love. Later, when you wish to re-open your inner door, ask it to open, and use your image to help you remember the feeling. You can do this any time: while driving, getting ready for sleep, or waiting for something, as well as in meditation or other more focused times of opening. Acknowledge whatever amount of opening that occurs, and know that it will grow.

If your inner door is not open, you are likely to be dependent on others for love. When you share love with others, love expands, but the basic knowledge of love is available to you at any time through your inner door. In fact, you cannot receive more love from others through your outer door than you receive from within through your inner door. Part of opening your inner door is loving yourself. Those who have difficulty loving themselves have difficulty receiving love from others.

Opening your outer door to love from others may inspire you to open your inner door, but your primary experience of love comes through your inner door. Love is already your reality, but if your inner door is closed, you do not know it. When you are joyously in love with another, there is a wonderful expansion of energy, but your partner is not the primary source of the love you feel. You primarily feel the love you are, coming forth. His love may help remind you of your potential to experience it, and your sharing with him may provide a larger space to contain it, but your experience is primarily of yourself. Your ability to have that experience is not dependent on any other person.

We suggest that you not give others or circumstances undue power over you. Take responsibility for having the experiences you choose to have. This includes making choices about what you open the outer door of your heart to. If it is not appropriate to be miserable in a particular situation, do not open your outer door to people or things that would bring misery to you. If, on the other hand, misery is appropriate for you, own your choice to feel miserable rather than being a victim of others or of situations.

There are times when it is appropriate to feel misery, such as, for example, if a loved one were just killed. However, if while feeling misery, you keep your inner door open to love, your misery will pass as quickly as possible under the circumstances. Many people do not fully feel their misery when it is appropriate to feel it. They close both their inner and outer doors. As a result, they carry the misery with them longer than otherwise would be necessary. Receiving love from others through your outer door can also help heal you, but your primary source of healing is through your inner door. If you are stuck in blaming others or circumstances for your experience, making them the primary source of your misery, you are not taking responsibility for being your own primary source of healing.

If a loved one were killed, it is not his death per se that causes you to feel as you do, but your experience of loss. Often people feel the need to rationalize their pain to make it more acceptable: "I feel bad only for others." When you truly feel for others, you feel for yourself, and you know that their pain is also yours.

There are those who are constantly feeling bad for others. Such people usually have open wounds in themselves that they have not yet taken responsibility for and allowed to heal. They project their pain onto others' pain. Conversely, those who feel little for others are not in their emotional bodies, and so feel little for themselves.

To feel is a gift. Be thankful for every feeling you have. Acknowledging your feelings, whatever they are, is the beginning of healing or expansion. Acknowledging confusion, for example, is the beginning of clarification. Acknowledging happiness causes happiness to increase in you.

It is truth that sets you free. You cannot become free on lies—for example, telling yourself that you are happy in a relationship if you are not. Nonetheless, there may be elements of the relationship that are good for you that you can acknowledge. Acknowledging them can help them expand.

The great goal is agape, unconditional love. A higher understanding of truth allows you to experience more love. Truth sets love free. Sometimes people feel that they are being truthful when they are merely being honest. Honesty is a part of truth, but truth is greater than honesty. People who say "I'm just being honest" may be missing other facts about the situation. The truth gives a balanced picture from a loving perspective. To approach the truth, honesty must be coupled with humility. Honesty with humility states, "This is how I see things right now. I'm open to seeing more." Honesty without humility imposes its view of the moment as being the final word. There is no final word. Reality is alive and ever-changing.

If you knew how much love is with you in every moment of your life, you would never again say that you are seeking love. You would instead say, "I am learning to open myself more and more to love." Love comes into your experience primarily through the inner door of your heart. It moves out through your outer door in fitting ways to those in the world with whom you have heart connections. It comes back in through it, not always in the ways you expect, from the heart response of others. In this way, a circuit of free-flowing energy is formed, making your heart healthy.

Heart disease is a leading cause of death. One reason is that love is not allowed to flow freely. When your heart is open and healthy, the rest of you tends to increase in health as well. Your body, for instance, feels better and tends to move toward greater health. You may, for example, have a desire to exercise because of the sense of vitality that arises from your heart. On the other hand, when you keep your body healthy and vibrant, your heart tends to feel safer to open. An open heart also gives rise to healthy thoughts, including greater understanding of why it is safe to open your heart. That reinforces the opening. Spiritual practices can fill your heart with a sense of peace, again bringing a greater sense of safety and well-being, causing it to open more, which in turn increases spiritual manifestation.

Everything you do can help you open the inner door of your heart—not just attending spiritual meetings, meditating, or reading metaphysical books. Playing a sport freely and joyfully can be just as effective. Spiritual teachings and practices can remind you to open the inner door, but they are not your source, any more than a lover is.

If you are in doubt as to what to do in any situation, look with your heart for what is true. You know if something is true because the truth sets you free. You experience a release, and your heart feels safer to open.

The highest truth is the simplest, and the truth is not merely an intellectual explanation; it resonates from your heart with your whole being. There is no need to take someone else's word for it when he says that something is true. You can validate it for yourself through your heart.

Your heart is beautiful. It is not merely a perfect heart that is beautiful. An imperfect heart seeking greater openness is beautiful, too. No one has a perfect heart, in the sense of having no unfinished business. This is not expected of you; you are not being "graded lower" for not having a perfect heart. You are not being graded at all.

There is much beauty in the imperfection of humanity seeking perfection. It is a long road, yet there is a part of you that is already perfect. It could be called your inner heart, that which is behind the inner door of your heart. It is perfect in the sense that it is not designed to have agendas or business to complete. The perfect part of you is not "better" or more valuable than the imperfect part. If there were not both a perfect and an imperfect part of you, you would not move or grow. The imperfect part of you is your raw material for expansion. Maybe you have more troubles and a larger backlog of issues to deal with than you would like, but you will catch up. You can take your time and enjoy the process. It is all right to be exactly where you are. You are in good hands: your own, to start with. 🍃

Chapter 11

LISTENING

L istening rarely occurs. Listening is not just hearing intellectually; it is receiving in your heart. Your heart is
your center where all the parts of your being can blend,
where your intellect can blend with your emotion and spirit.
When you listen with your heart, you are receiving another
with your wholeness. The fact that your heart is your center is
illustrated by the fact that your heart chakra is also your center
chakra, the fourth out of seven—there are three below and
three above.

Listening involves not only receiving, but comprehending.
Of course, you cannot comprehend if you do not first receive.
Even when you do receive, your comprehension will be faulty
if you translate what you receive through inaccurate beliefs. It
is wise not to jump to conclusions about what you are receiving. Take your time. Listen not only for what you are receiving,
but also to your reactions. They can alert you to beliefs you
may wish to change.

True listening penetrates. Many people think that only action penetrates, but listening can be as powerful as acting.
Listening is a function of female energy, being receptive. Acting is a function of male energy. The Orient, being more
feminine, makes greater use of meditation and other forms of
listening than the Occident.

Meditation can be an excellent way to develop the ability
to listen. If you listen in meditation, you can hear things you
never heard before. You might say, "Well, it's just my imagi-
nation." It is true that everything you perceive is of necessity
translated by your consciousness. Even in human language, in
which certain definitions are generally agreed upon, communication is subject to the hearer's translation. Many
misunderstandings result because people do not translate in the
same way. But even if you inaccurately translate what you hear

in meditation, it does not necessarily mean that it is a figment of your fancy.

One reason that listening is difficult, especially for those in the Occident, is that activity is so highly emphasized, resulting in imbalance. Listening is often seen as doing nothing. As a result, the intellect is trained to be occupied with acting. A good exercise is to listen to your mind. It is probably filled with what you have done and are going to do—occupied with action. When acting is balanced with listening, acting becomes more efficient. In listening to your thoughts, you can readily observe how many are repetitious and unnecessary. In balance, you can attain mastery, doing what is necessary in a streamlined manner. A balanced person lives with grace. There is a rhythm to his movements.

There is a time to listen, a time to act, and a time to rest. You are learning many lessons by living in a society that emphasizes action so much. Action is not wrong, just as listening is not right. They are two aspects of one thing. Action springs from listening—they are not separable, just as words spring from silence, and are not separable. Without silence between words, words would be one unending sound. Action without listening results in a similar blur. Beautiful listening is required for beautiful action. Through this channel, we speak slowly, and the silences between words are pronounced. During the silences we listen to those present. You do not have to speak slowly to do this, but sometimes it helps.

If you love yourself, you listen to yourself. Your voice is plural: there are many parts of you that speak to you. You know this if you stub your toe—your toe speaks to you. But there are various levels of self speaking to you continually. Sometimes the only way they can get your attention is through your dreams. If you have nightmares, it is often an indication that you are not listening to a part of yourself that has urgently been trying to get your attention. It says, "Maybe if I scare him, he'll listen."

Most parents do not even attempt to listen to their children. They want their children to listen to them, but they do not

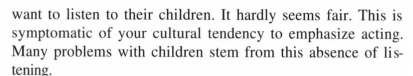

want to listen to their children. It hardly seems fair. This is symptomatic of your cultural tendency to emphasize acting. Many problems with children stem from this absence of listening.

Love is the great goal. To love, one must listen.

When you listen internally, how can you distinguish between what you should and should not act on? If I hear that I should shoot somebody, I don't act on it, but some people do. Where do you draw the line?

We mentioned that listening is made up of receiving and comprehending, and that the translation of what you receive might be faulty. Listen for what is underneath the impulse to shoot someone, for example. There is something that needs to be done, but it is probably not shooting someone. Obviously, there is great fear or anger present behind such a voice. By truly listening to this voice, you bring it into your understanding heart, surrounding it with love and acceptance. Then you see what is truly needed. You act on what you receive when you listen, but consciously and intelligently, not in a knee-jerk manner.

What can you do when trying to communicate with people who can't or don't listen?

First, be very clear in your communication with them, because if you are not, they are not likely to hear you. Second, work even more on your own listening. If you listen intently to others, you tend to evoke listening in them, although it may not be to the extent you would like. Looking at them in the eyes can sometimes help make contact.

When you listen fully, you receive more than just the words spoken. For instance, you receive the emotions behind the words. They can be either congruous or incongruous with the words spoken. If they are incongruous, you might be wise to question the person about the discrepancy you perceive, so that your communication can be clear. Two identical state-

ments can mean different things with different emotional content.

You can also receive through body language and other
paths of communication. Even subtle scents given off during
communication can provide you with information. It is a matter
of how open you are to receive all that is being given, and your
ability to comprehend it. No matter how open your listening is,
you can always open more.

*It seems that when I am able to listen to someone, they can
speak. When I can't, they can't. What I am receptive to hearing
often determines what can happen in my space.*

Yes, it is true that what can be said is often determined by the
depth of listening present. One reason we are so careful to develop the atmosphere in the groups to which we speak is that if
there is not adequate listening, there is not much we can say. If
we just started rattling on from the beginning, we could no
doubt entertain, but there would not be depth.

If you have something difficult to say to someone, it is
easier if he is receptive. Sometimes you dread having to bring
up an unpleasant subject and it turns out to be relatively easy;
other times people make difficult what could be easy.

When you are with someone who is truly receptive to you,
you often surpass your expectations. A performer finds that
certain audiences draw his best from him, because they have
the room to receive his best. We mentioned that listening can
be as penetrating as action. The audience's listening reaches
into the performer's core, drawing from him his full potential.
Another audience with less receptivity can make his work difficult.

The same is true for healers, and in every walk of life.
Listening is quite potent. Although traditional psychotherapy is
often not as effective as it could be, people are sometimes
willing to pay large sums of money for it. Part of the reason is
that most psychotherapists know how to listen, at least after a

fashion. People can sometimes be healed by listening alone. A block can be removed when there is a place for it to go.

Could listening replace active methods of healing?

Since listening and action are not separable, listening could not replace action. Listening properly brings forth appropriate action. For example, a body worker listening to his client does a better job of discovering the most effective means of working on him. Listening is not better than action, although a healer who does not listen is quite limited. We are speaking of listening now because this society knows more about action than about listening.

If you experience healing simply because someone listens to you, you were probably in a state of imbalance in which you greatly needed someone to listen to you. Once the need is filled and the balance restored, the person listening to you will probably have something to say. You become the listener, until the balance again shifts, triggering more for you to say. It goes back and forth. If a therapist listens without acting, whether through words, movement, energy, or through another means, an exchange does not occur.

I've heard that men and women listen differently. Women, when they listen, are more supportive—they nod and are more responsive, while men listen silently. Also, men interrupt women more often than vice versa.

Not every man is higher in male energy, but being in a male body, male energy is emphasized. Male energy is more about action. It is therefore not surprising that men have more of a tendency to interrupt and not listen as well as women. However, a man who has integrated his male and female energies tends to be a better listener than one who has not. Men more often need to be taught how to listen, just as women more often need to be taught how to act. Of course, both men and women have much to learn about both acting and listening.

To foster better listening with another person, you can make an agreement that you will each wait an entire second after the other has finished speaking before chiming in, just to make sure that he is finished. In addition, you can repeat back, without criticism, what you heard and see if it is correct. You can also request that he tell you what he heard you say.

Listening is a beautiful experience. When you have that experience, you can sometimes inspire the desire for it in another.

Listening can also be frightening. You can hear things, especially about yourself, that you don't want to hear.

It is true that sometimes you have to be courageous to listen. Your love of the truth has to be greater than your fear of it. When you first start to listen to yourself, you tend to receive what is most blatant. As you continue, you receive more subtle information, which can shed light on what is more blatant, making it less frightening.

Is listening to your inner child, for example, different from listening to your essence or your body?

The quality in listening would be the same. You would simply be tuning in to a different place on the dial, so to speak. If you wished to listen to your body, you would sense your body's vibration; you would feel your body. Your body feels different from your essence. With practice, you learn what that difference is.

How can you distinguish between listening with your heart and listening with your mind?

Listening with your heart has both intellectual and emotional components that are integrated. If you listen only with your intellect, you receive only intellectually. If you listen only emotionally, you receive only emotionally. Wisdom results from integrating them. In your society, if there is any listening, it is usually intellectual. However, if you are listening to your own emotions, you are better able to receive others' emotions. Emotions convey different information than the intellect. If you have been listening only with your intellect, you might want to focus on listening emotionally for a while as a means of learning to listen with your whole being through your heart.

MEDITATION

Listen to your body. Listen to your emotions. How are they contained in your body? Listen to your thoughts. Do they sit well in your body, or are they awkward there? Listen to your essence. Feel how it is larger than your body, your emotions, and your thoughts. Feel enveloped in it.

Listen to the sweetness of the Tao, the ground of all being. Receive and translate correctly its vibration. 🐚

❧ Chapter 12 ❧

COMMUNICATING YOUR WHOLE BEING

To communicate fully requires your entire being. True communication is not merely of your thoughts, but is an interchange of your whole being with the one with whom you are communicating. If you are trapped in a narrow part of yourself, you cannot experience the fullness of communication. Loving yourself is loving the whole of your being. What you love, you include. What you include, you can communicate.

During moments of silence, forms of communication other than through sound can take place. The overreliance on communication through words is one of humanity's greatest limitations. Having only words with which to communicate would be like having only pencils with which to make art. You can make lovely drawings with pencils, but they lack the full expressiveness possible in art. Some people think that they are inadequate communicators because they are not particularly verbal. It is good to be capable of using words to communicate. Nevertheless, there are many other avenues of communication. Body language, facial expressions, gestures, and other actions are obvious examples of nonverbal physical communication.

You can also communicate in nonphysical ways. Telepathy, the transference of thought, is an example of intellectual communication not using sound. A less focused kind of telepathy occurs when you think of someone and then receive a phone call from him shortly thereafter; he received your thought of him, but not necessarily what you wanted to communicate. Telepathy can also be more specific, but that is rare between people.

The most unrecognized medium of communication is pure energy.[6] Einstein said that $E = mc^2$, that energy converts to matter and vice versa. Energy also permeates matter. You are

---

[6]See also the author's upcoming Summerjoy Michael book *Opening to Healing Energy.*

communicating through your energy continually. The Tao is the source of all energy, but there are infinite variations in energy's manifestation. Your energy is as unique as your fingerprints and far more significant. It communicates your beliefs and feelings. Others are usually not able to interpret it consciously, but some part of them recognizes more or less accurately what your energy communicates.

It can be valuable to take stock of what you communicate through your energy. You might ask what it feels like to others to be in your energy. For example, does it stimulate, calm, or both? Most importantly, is it a healing force?

Changing your personal energy is both a long process and something you can do effectively in a moment. Your energy springs primarily from your intent. In any moment that your intent changes or clarifies, your energy shifts. If, for example, you are vacuuming your rug and your only intent is to complete that job, your energy reflects that focus. You have a narrow experience of your total energy; only what relates to your intent to vacuum the rug comes forth. If your awareness opens and your intent becomes to fill the rug and the rest of the room with golden light as you vacuum the rug well, your energy shifts to accommodate that intent. This is why we say that changing your energy can be done quickly. However, if you have not had much practice holding this larger intent in your awareness, it tends to snap back to the more narrow one. Over time you can cultivate the ability to keep it more open. Also, the parts of you not in agreement with your larger intent surface, and need to be worked with. The ultimate goal is to communicate your whole being through your energy.

EXERCISE

With a partner, sit quietly and communicate as much of your whole being as possible, receiving your partner's energy at the same time. Notice what is communicated that could not be communicated through words or in other ways. When you are done, discuss your experience.

You might experience some awkwardness in such an exercise. People often hide behind words because communicating in larger ways exposes them more. Yet if you are to have rewarding communication, it must be open and expansive.

If you try to communicate, you limit your communication, but if you relax and let yourself be with the other person, communication is easier. Those who flood others with words are sometimes attempting to make up for a lack of ability to be with others. They sense that there should be some communication, but communication is impossible if you are not sharing your being.

When you wish to communicate with someone, first establish a connection with him, if you do not have one already, so you are being with him. Listen for his presence rather than being too full of what you want to say. It will make your verbal communication easier and more potent. Eye contact can facilitate this, or just seeing his body. Establishing this connection can happen in just a moment or two.

Your listening to someone else's communication is itself a form of communication with him. It is saying, "I value you. I hear you. I know who you are. I understand what you are saying." And perhaps "I love you." Through listening, your beings can connect and part of your thought is communicated, so that less needs to be said in words.

Communication is a prerequisite for blending. If you cannot give yourself and receive others, which is what communication is, you cannot blend with someone else. There are many avenues through which you can give yourself and receive others, such as time, money, possessions, words, creativity, and thought. How easily you give and receive these things can be symbolic of how easily you give yourself and receive others. Many people give and receive in a limited way. You may have relatives who give you things but not kind words (or the reverse).

You can only give freely what you are not attached to. Attachment is motivated by fear. Generally, you are attached to what you believe is scarce. Those who give freely of their time, money, love, and so forth, usually believe that these things are abundant. How much you can give is more a function of your belief than of how much you actually have. Being unattached to money, for instance, does not imply that you simply give it all away, although someone unattached to money can give it freely when that is appropriate. A spendthrift may be just as attached to money as a miser is. Both are motivated by fear. A spendthrift may spend lavishly because he fears that others will not otherwise like or respect him, or to try to fill an inner void. That is not the same as spending money neutrally or joyfully simply for the value received.

Just as you cannot give freely what you do not feel you abundantly have, you cannot communicate what you do not include as part of yourself. Ultimately, everything is part of you. Most people at one time or another suffer from loneliness. Loneliness is fundamentally a longing for the experience of wholeness. Intrinsic to it is the belief that you are separate from other parts of the whole.

To illustrate wholeness, let's look at your body. Obviously, your body has form. The form of your heart is not the same as the form of the blood it pumps. However, your heart could not live without the blood in it. They are separate but not separate at the same time: they are part of the same whole.

To take the analogy one step further, your skin is apparently separate from the air touching it, but the air is just a different form of matter. Who is to say that it is not still part of your body? In fact, there is air inside your body. You breathe the air, and it breathes you. There is no place you could physically go without air. You share air with the rest of the planet, just as your heart shares its blood with the rest of your body, but the air is part of who you are.

Moving from your skin through the adjacent air, you can reach another person's skin. Are you separate from that other person? You are connected to the same air. He may just be a different form of you. Within your body, at one point your form is your heart, and at a slightly different point your form is your blood. On a larger scale, perhaps at one point your form is

John Smith, and at a slightly different point your form is Jane Jones. Where do you end? Where do you start, for that matter? Ideas about ending and starting are conveniences. They do not relate to Reality with a capital "R." Again, $E = mc^2$. Things can change but they cannot end or begin.

There is only the All That Is, which divides and multiplies itself, you might say, for its own amusement. All communication is ultimately the Tao talking to itself, in countless ways.

What happens to your energy when you're in a situation you don't want to be in?

If your intent is just to get by, that is reflected in your energy. On the other hand, if you choose to be fully there no matter what initiated your being there, you can develop an intent that allows you to manifest a more expansive energy. We are assuming that leaving is not an option.

Your energy springs from whatever aspects of your wholeness you allow to manifest. You are constantly making choices about this. The artistry of living effectively involves making the best choices you can. There are times when it is appropriate to access a so-called negative part of yourself, especially if you are working with it to heal it or integrate it into the rest of you. However, if, for instance, you inappropriately manifest a mean-spirited part of you, letting it take control, that is communicated in your energy. All the parts of you are valid, but to be an effective artist of living, you need to be conscious of which color you paint on which canvas, to make an analogy.

When you do not direct your energy through a specific intent, your energy reflects your habitual intent, which is formed by the sum of your parts. We might call that energy your "aggregate energy." Over time, you can change it by changing the intent of your parts.

For example, if you heal that mean-spirited part of yourself rather than unconsciously letting it take control, it now has a loving intent to contribute to the whole of you. That alters your habitual intent, lifting your aggregate energy. As you choose to live primarily from the most enlightened parts of yourself, you can heal those that are less enlightened. To enlighten is to make light. This is a never-ending process. There is no limit to how high you can lift your aggregate energy. This is the essential process of life.

Perhaps you have known someone who has a problem with substance abuse. If you knew him before he had the problem, you have probably observed a decrease in the quality of his energy. When he begins to take control of the problem and return to a more conscious way of living, his aggregate personal energy will begin to elevate once more.

Most people have experienced many other lifetimes and planets. Your deeper personal energies have developed much more slowly than those that reflect the immediate issues you are dealing with. Who you are in this sense is not changed much by anything you have done in this lifetime, let alone by an error you made last week. You are like a very old tree that develops a new ring every year. What you experience now is on the surface of your being. It is part of the ring you are forming now. It is important, but do not overrate it. You are the whole tree, not just the outer ring. In other words, you are your whole being, not just your surface personality. As you live from your wholeness, you can communicate it, through your energy and all you do.

You are a remarkable, magnificent being having experience in this little place called earth. Rest in who you are. Trust who you are. It makes your life much more enjoyable. Allow yourself to fully communicate who you are to others. You are always communicating at least part of who you are anyway. Perhaps sometimes you unconsciously communicate parts of yourself that you would rather not, but who you are is beautiful. Yes, there are parts of you that need healing, but relative to the whole of you, all of them are minor. To heal is to make whole, to integrate these parts into your beautiful wholeness.

The reason we are nonjudgmental is that we see your wholeness. There is nothing you could do, whether it springs from love or fear, that could eclipse who you are. If you know this about yourself, you can communicate the enormous, magnificent, unlimited being you are. There is much we could say about techniques of communicating clearly through words with others. Most people need a great deal of work on such techniques, but important as they are, they are not a substitute for this basic awareness.

Communication is a step away from communion. Communion is a step away from the Tao. The physical plane provides many lessons that are quite useful in developing the capacity to communicate and ultimately merge your whole being with others. ᗰ

Chapter 13

FRIENDSHIP

It is a happy occasion to meet with friends. When friends gather, an atmosphere of warmth and intimacy is generated. You do not have to know everything about another person to know that you are friends. Have you ever met someone for the first time and felt as if you had always known him? You did know him; you just did not know his present personality structure. Personalities are important, but they are not the whole being.

Through friendship you learn many of your most important life lessons. You will probably be mated to only one person at a time, if one, but you probably have many friends. Friendships are excellent opportunities to practice unconditional acceptance, or at least a high degree of tolerance.

What is the difference between a friend and an acquaintance? You might say that a friend is someone for whom you are willing to go out on a limb. It is someone you wish to understand, someone you care about, and who is significant in your life. Acquaintances are all the others you know. You are familiar with them, but you have no aspirations toward intimacy with them. By intimacy we do not, of course, necessarily refer to physical sex, but to the intercourse of self. There are those who have known one another for many years and have spent much time together but are acquaintances rather than friends. In fact, some people have no friends at all.

People tend to choose friends who are similar in many ways to themselves. Those with whom you share a high number of similarities are generally more comfortable for you. However, those who are friends only with people like themselves may feel that their kind of people is the most acceptable. They are limiting their opportunities to practice acceptance. On the other hand, if you genuinely accept your similar friends, you are practicing self-acceptance. Sometimes people project what they find unpalatable in themselves on their friends.

Those who have difficulty maintaining friendships often do this.

It is rarer for people to have a majority of friends who are different from themselves, but that does occur. Such people may feel that who they are is unacceptable, and may wish to be like those other people. On the other hand, much is learned through diversity. If you have a high degree of exposure to other ways of being, you are not as likely to be locked into one.

Some people like to have many friends, while others like to have few. Those with few may have chosen to work more alone in this lifetime. They may also lack social skills; if that is the case, they often long to improve them, and may be attracted to those who have them. Still others value their friendships and want to devote themselves deeply to a few. They feel that they would spread themselves too thin with many. Each person has a unique way of being, including a way of being a friend.

If you would like to have more friends, ask yourself what you have to offer your friends and what you would like from them. If you seek friends who share common interests, you might deliberately put yourself in more situations where you can meet such people. This, by the way, also goes for those who are seeking a mate.

You may be hesitant to make the first move to develop friendship, fearing rejection. If you lack communication skills, you can practice them. For example, if you are shy about approaching someone, you might prepare yourself with ten different things you could say to break the ice. We suggest a high number such as ten so you can be flexible in your approach and intuitively sense in the moment which ice-breaker is most appropriate. If you have only one or two prepared and neither is appropriate, you will feel even more awkward.

The most social activity is eating. You can always invite someone to share a meal with you. You might quake at the thought if you are not sure that you can sustain a conversation. If so, think about what you would like to know about him. Often others are delighted at your interest in them. You can also prepare what you would like to have him know about you.

If you are not confident in your verbal skills, you might choose instead to do something together, perhaps something athletic. Just going to a movie will not give you much opportunity to interact, whereas, for example, going boating or bowling together would. Think about what would be most comfortable for you.

If deliberately cultivating friendship is new to you, you might feel uncomfortable whatever you do. If you take a step, applaud yourself for doing so, and do not judge yourself for your mistakes. If you seem to be compatible with the other person, you might, before you part company, set another time to get together. That would save you from having to get up the courage to make another phone call, if that is a problem for you.

If you have as many friendships as you desire, yet find them often disappointing or confusing, examine them more deeply. Do you always wait for your friends to call you? Or are you the one who always calls? Do you classify yourself as a bad letter-writer, or a good one? Which of your present friendships do you enjoy the most? Which do you enjoy the least? Why? Answering these questions will help you develop a strategy for creating more of the types of friendships you would like to have.

If spirituality is important in your life, your closest friends are likely to also have such an interest. That makes sense, since you share the most with those who have common priorities. However, someone who does not appear to be on a spiritual path could still be a good friend. It is important to be able to see beyond the surface. Some truly spiritual people have no conscious knowledge of metaphysical or spiritual principles, but their values may actually be quite harmonious with yours. By the same token, people interested in metaphysics are not necessarily spiritual.

Your spiritual path may involve a particular organization or teaching, such as the Michael teachings. But the organization or teaching is not the path itself—it is a tool you are using, and someone's lack of interest in it should not alone be grounds for rejecting friendship with him. To make an analogy, if you have a passion for stamp collecting, and someone else has no interest in it, you would probably not exclude him from your life for that reason. Although common interests and involvements can be helpful in a friendship, common values are more important.

Friendships have many different purposes. Some friendships are lifelong; others are for a short period. It is important to know when to let go of them. Some people abandon friendships at the first sign of difficulty. This can be an indication of undeveloped skills in hurdling obstacles or simply fear of dealing with them. Others hang onto friendships at all costs. There is a middle ground. Friendships that become dormant are not really lost. Whatever is between you and another person on an essence level is still there. You need not fear letting go of the form of the friendship—it may resume later anyway. On the other hand, running away from difficulties can be at the cost of important life lessons.

If you are in doubt whether a friendship is worth continuing to work on, you might ask yourself several questions: "Has it become one-sided?" "What value does it provide in my life?" "What would be my motivation for ending it or for trying to make it continue?" And so forth. If you entered a friendship on a certain basis—for example, trying to save the other person—and you are no longer trying to save people, examine whether the friendship can be given a different basis. If your friend is still looking for you to save him, and will not accept who you are or how you wish to be in your friendship now, it is probably time to let it go.

How is the interaction and communication between two friends different on an essence level than on a personality level?

On an essence level, you generally take a lighter and more objective view of life. For instance, if on a personality level you are arguing with a friend over something minor, you are likely to see a lot of humor in that on an essence level.

When you wake up remembering a dream involving a certain friend, might that be recall of an essence communication?

It may be essence communication, or it may be symbolic (or both). Dreams that are evidence of essence communication are generally more realistic. Symbolic dreams tend to be more sur-realistic.

You need many kinds of friendship. Not everyone in your life needs to think that you are perfection personified. Not everyone needs to be a nurturer for you. Most people need a friend or two who tell it like it is, as they see it. You need people who help you laugh and thereby gain perspective on your life. You need people who bring out the child in you, with whom you can play. You need people upon whose shoulders you can cry or lean occasionally. Many people expect all these qualities from their mates. It is a rare individual who can do all those things for you. Even if your mate does admirably, you may not want to continually ask that much of him.

Sometimes people are jealous of their mate's friends. It can be easily recognized that such jealousy springs from insecurity. If you feel pangs of jealousy when your mate is close to other people, you might be relying too heavily on your mate to fill your needs. Perhaps you could fill more of them yourself, or cultivate your own friendships more. You might also examine your fundamental beliefs about life: Is the world a place of lack, as far as you are concerned? Do you feel that there is not enough love and attention to go around? Or do you believe that the world is a generous place, full of all the love and friendship you need and desire? The latter is true, but if you believe otherwise, you do not experience it that way.

Friendship can provide much richness and support in life. No one is meant to go through life doing everything himself. There is no reason each person cannot have the support he needs from other people. ❧

Chapter 14

INTERACTING WITH OTHERS

[Mostly to Specific Individuals]

RELATIONSHIP WITH THE UNIVERSE

Your relationships with others, especially with those to whom you are closest, have much to do with your relationship with the universe as a whole. The universe is usually thought of as being "out there," but you are part of it; the universe is "in here," too.[7]

Every relationship gives you an opportunity to learn something more about the whole in which all of us live.

WHY PEOPLE ARE IN YOUR LIFE

There are many possible reasons certain people are in your life. You may have karmic ties[8] with them, or may have made agreements before the lifetime began to accomplish specific tasks. You attract some people because of similar or complementary beliefs or patterns of behavior. You can also attract people who are opposite from you in order to balance yourself.

You have known most of the important people in your life during other lifetimes. You are like a member of a large theatre repertory company that puts on different plays with the same pool of actors. Your company is analogous to your spiritual family or circle of friends. Every actor is not in every play, but eventually, you work with most of the actors in your company several times. Bit players may be hired from outside to fill in the ranks. Occasionally a guest artist is brought in as well. But the bulk of the plays are performed by your company.

---

[7]A reminder: when passages in a subchapter are from different source material, they are separated by double spacing.

[8]Karmic ties are debts from past lives caused by violating the rights of others. Murder, for instance, is usually karmic.

MORALITY

Morality is often merely a fear-based belief system rather than a loving desire to interact with the rest of life appropriately. We would say that true morality is the desire to impact what is around you in a way that is constructive, or at least not destructive.

APPROPRIATENESS

Appropriateness can be defined as behavior that is both an honest expression of your feelings and considerate of how it affects others.

You cannot do anything about how another person chooses to express his feelings. Therefore, the only appropriateness of interest to you is your own. Fretting over what you cannot control is a stress you do not need.

How can you learn to recognize when you are expressing something inappropriately?

When you are expressing something appropriately, it feels right and is usually easy to say or do. It is like going with the grain when sanding wood. You might be nervous on one level, yet you do not feel that you are forcing something on the situation. The power within you supports that expression. The reverse is true when you are expressing something inappropriately.

How do you know whether you are giving too much?

Again, if you are giving the right amount, the giving usually moves easily and makes contact. If you are giving too much, you might have the feeling of being out of control, a little like a roller coaster going off its tracks. Listen to how it feels. As long as it feels appropriate, it probably is.

    If you are in doubt as to whether the other person fully welcomes what you are giving, you might ask him. He will usually tell you. If he is trying to be polite, you can usually figure out what he really feels through his tone of voice, body language, and so forth.

What if someone likes what you're giving, but doesn't reciprocate?

Unless there is both giving and receiving, there is not a complete circuit, and the natural flow stops. Without some form of receiving, at some point what you are giving will not move easily, and will not feel right.

What you receive is not always in kind. For example, in raising children, what you receive from them is obviously of a different nature from what you give them. Part of what you receive may be your growth in raising them. At times it may appear that you are not receiving anything of value from them, but over the long run, there will probably be a complete circuit. In any case, becoming a parent was your choice.

In relationships in which you are repaying a karmic debt, the giving, although not necessarily pleasant, is completing a circuit begun in the past. Therefore, your giving still moves easily and somehow feels right. What you receive is the erasure of the debt.

However, when someone is happily "sponging off" you, in most cases it does not feel right. If you continue to give against the flow, you are probably receiving an unhealthy "payoff" psychologically.

BEING FRANK

It is difficult to be intimately involved with people who are not capable of much understanding. However, it can be good work to be frank and ask them to stretch. They may benefit from their association with you even if they kick and squeal for the moment. We suggest that you stay on the high road with them, remaining uninvolved with their tempests and not taking them too seriously.

EXPLANATION

Some people believe that explanation can solve every problem. Let's look at an example taking this belief to its absurd but logical extreme. Suppose that a political prisoner holding this belief is about to be executed, and tries to sit down with the officer and explain that this is really not appropriate behavior. He offers him a historical perspective, assuming that once the officer understood the context of his actions, he would say, "Go. I made a mistake." Of course, that would not be the likely result.

Explanation is not an all-purpose panacea. Sometimes, to best offer healing, a less direct approach is needed.

CHEMISTRY

The situation you describe is one of temporarily uncomfortable chemistry between two growing people. You tend to take a more positive approach, while your friend tends to emphasize the negative. Be careful not to make him wrong—there are no villains in this story. Your positivity is as uncomfortable for him as his negativity is for you.

Examine the source of your positivity. When it is fully coming from love, you will be neutral about other people's reactions to it. Being positive to ensure that other people are kind to you is as much fear-based as his being negative to keep himself insulated from other people. You are truly coming from different places here. Tolerate his place, and you will grow.

RECEIVING

You perceive the help of others as incurring a burdensome debt to repay. When you receive freely what others wish to give freely, they are blessed by the joy of giving.

BEING LOVED BY OTHERS

You can have many shortcomings and still be beautiful and totally worth loving as you are. Your sense of worth does not have to be wrapped up in your shortcomings. Do you suppose that those who are loved by many people are without flaws? Who on earth or even on the higher planes of creation is without flaws? The goal is not to become a static image of perfection, like a statue. Just keep moving in your process, and you are perfect in the view of all those who truly love.

MAINTAINING INNER PEACE

How do you keep inner peace, confidence, and love when everyone around you is angry?

You might first ask yourself why you are in a situation in which everyone around you is angry. Others may be mirroring unacknowledged anger in you. By acknowledging and releasing it, you may be able to change your environment. If you are in a stressful work situation that breeds short tempers, you might consider whether you wish to remain there, or if some changes could be made.

The key to maintaining inner peace, confidence, and love under stress is to create a strong atmosphere of those qualities around you when you are not under stress. There are many ways to do this: Take time for yourself on a regular basis to do things you enjoy, whether it is shopping, meditating, singing, or going to a park. Surround yourself with beautiful things. When you are around angry people, take breaks during which you revitalize your atmosphere—you might, for example, go out for a walk. As with anything else, the more you practice creating and sustaining inner peace, the better you get at it.

Maintain a clear intent not to participate in other people's reactions. Choose your responses carefully, and remember your sense of humor.

BEING ANOTHER—AN EXERCISE

For five minutes, pretend that you are the other person to whom you wish to relate better. See if you can think his thoughts, and more important, feel his feelings. You might even see if you can move like him. If you find this difficult, pay closer attention to him when you are next with him. You can try the exercise again afterward.

This can be a powerful exercise. You probably know in theory that all people are one. As you do this exercise, you begin to recognize core resonances, and see that many differences between people are on the level of style and imprinting. Not far below the surface, there are more similarities than you might have imagined. It is one thing to intellectually understand this, and another to know it.

IN GOOD RELATIONSHIP—A MEDITATION

See yourself as being in good relationship with everyone in your life. Think of a few of those people individually and see yourself as being in good relationship with them. Now see yourself as being in good relationship with the sun, the moon, the stars, and the earth. And now see yourself as being in good relationship with yourself. 🐏

Chapter 15

DIFFERENT WAYS OF LOVING

The months June and July each have particular qualities that most find beautiful, yet they are different from one another. In much of the Northern Hemisphere, June still has a flavor of spring, although it is generally becoming hot, whereas July has the bona fide flavor of summer. October smells of piles of leaves; November, of frostiness; February, of unending quiet; and April, of new birth.

There is something beautiful about every point in the cycle. You might say that the qualities we described are positive sides of those months. July can scorch; February can be bitterly cold. These are negative sides.

This analogy gives you an idea of the infinite variety of ways love can manifest: some people love in a way more akin to April; others, to September; still others, to February. Using another analogy, some people love more in the manner of Venus; others, in the manner of Mars. Mars loves with an intense focus; Venus, with soft caresses. Both are needed. There is no wrong way of loving, but as mentioned, there are positive and negative sides to everything. The positive sides reveal part of the true nature of love; the negative sides reveal those same qualities distorted by fear.

What makes for beauty in you and anywhere is love. Love is the source of beauty. A beautiful person is one in whom love is much in evidence. Love manifests in an infinite number of ways. There is no one proper expression for it. You are encouraged to find your own way of manifesting what love is. When you do this, you expand love's scope.

Love is not necessarily dominantly sweet. Love can be sweet, but it can be pungent as well. Not every flower smells like a rose, but each flower's scent is beautiful. All flowers, by the way, have a scent, even if your nose cannot smell it.

You have a way of loving that is right for you. You do not need to copy another person's way. You may wish to do so temporarily as a means of expanding your repertoire of loving behaviors, but if you are to know yourself, eventually you must find your own way of loving.

Sometimes people are disappointed at another person's way of loving. Perhaps his expression of it is distorted in some way by mixed motivations. He may not be expressing very much love at all. But many times people are confused because they look for a particular way of loving, Venus's way, for example, when the other person loves like Mars. It is the course of wisdom to learn to respect the way others give love, and to honor your own way. Some people are naturally sweet when they love. Some people love with much humor, while others love with great sincerity. Still others love with nobility of intent. Some people feel that to love is to do, while others feel that to love is to say. Those who express love primarily through words may feel that if someone does not say the words "I love you," he does not love. Although we encourage people to have the ability to verbalize their feelings, if you dismiss another person based on his inability to say that he loves you, you are not recognizing his totality.

As mentioned, mixed motivations frequently enter in, and these too are confusing. Usually love, as it is experienced on the physical plane, is not whole; people hold pieces of love back. People act hurtfully as well as lovingly. If someone acts hurtfully to you, it has more to do with his own lack of evolvement than with anything you have done. If you wish to see him in a balanced way, you must also acknowledge his expressions of loving intent. Doing so can increase them. Acknowledging expressions of loving intent is also vital when you are working with children—and with yourself: acknowledge your own loving intent as well as the pieces of love you hold back. An expression of loving intent is beautiful, true, sound, balanced, strong, clear, and wise. Expanding your ability to love is the highest goal you can strive for.

As part of the human tendency to focus on the negative, people often acknowledge what is not of loving intent in others, but little of what is. Even if a couple is finding creative ways to resolve their differences rather than fighting continu-ally, what is all their effort for if they are not also acknowledging expressions of loving intent in each other?

It is true that if you try to repress what bothers you in an-other person, it becomes harder to see his fine qualities. But if you see an unending parade of irritating or uncomfortable qualities, there is a good chance that either you are in the wrong relationship, or you have not learned to see expressions of loving intent. If you cannot see them in your partner, you probably cannot see them in yourself. If you cannot see them in yourself, consider the people who taught you how to see your-self. These were likely your parents. Were they able to see love around themselves? If not, have compassion for them, and re-alize that you have to learn how to do this on your own. This, you might say, is Spirituality 101.

Many people think that they are spiritual because they have an intellectual understanding of metaphysics. Although we do not discourage a study of metaphysics, you might say that to be spiritual is to love. Love in the way that is natural for you. Do not reject love simply because you cannot love in the way others do, and do not reject the love of others because they do not love in your way. Find your own core of love and learn to bring it to the surface.

MEDITATION

Ask to travel into your core of love. Be there now. If you do not feel anything, that is all right—imagine what it would be like if you were there. Use similes to describe it to yourself. You might say that it is like a waterfall, or like the white stream behind a jet in the sky. You might say that it is the color of a lily pad, or the texture of a leaf. Take a moment and get to know it.

When you said to ask to travel, I had the sensation of falling. When you said, "Be there," I landed with a bump. It was beautiful, so white that it was almost silvery. It had a crystal-

line quality to it. It was warm and soft. I got images of a mother's breast or a baby's skin. It was that kind of warmth. There was a heartbeat, and an incredible amount of loving acceptance, both within, because I was surrounded by it, and then outside. It was very beautiful.

My core of love was light and clear crystal, extremely familiar and comfortable. It brought back memories of a series of meditations I did about ten years ago in which I kept seeing stained glass with the message, "Don't go through the colors. Just go through the clear."

Much to my surprise, I saw powerful colorations of blue, white, and black, and heard a voice that was dynamic, powerful, and energetic.

Quite different, isn't it, from what the other two shared, yet valid.

Mine was a water lily. It didn't go anywhere. I was struck by the consistency of it. It was very simple. I felt the sun crowning me, and a gentle rocking motion that carried me away. It was very pleasant. It took me a long time to get there. I had to collect pieces of myself, but when I arrived, it was quite easy. It was like plunking myself down there. There was a lot of giggling. That was the height of the experience.

That is a key for you, isn't it? Perhaps, when you are looking for a way to extend your core of love to someone, you can do so with humor.

I felt the sun also, as if I were sunbathing at the beach. It felt very good.

My core felt kind of soft and mushy, like pizza dough. A circle, and the words "agape" and "comfort," kept showing up. It felt kinesthetic, touchy.

My experience was different: clouds and cool mist, as opposed to the warmth of the sun and lots of light.

This suggests to us that your way of loving is refreshing, like the ocean spray in your face, enlivening as opposed to a more soothing and relaxing way of loving. If you are overheated, there is nothing more welcome than a cool mist!

This is a simple exercise, but if you can remember what it felt like when you tapped into your core of love, it will be easier to do it again.

If you were not given enough love as a child, how does that distort your ability to love? How is that resolved?

You may have difficulty connecting with your core of love, because you do not know what love feels like. However, sometimes that lack motivates you to dig deeper within—you become ennobled instead of hardened. You may have come into the world with a strong connection to your core of love. You can then use external deprivation to strengthen it further. By maintaining or reestablishing that connection without outer reinforcement, you realize that your core of love cannot be taken from you. The harder it is to win this knowledge, the more precious and strong it is when you find it. There were probably others along the way who reminded you of your core of love, in addition to inner guidance coaching you.

Being connected with your core of love does not necessarily prevent you from being wounded, nor does it automatically heal past wounds. However, taking responsibility to heal them strengthens your connection, which, in turn, makes it easier to heal them, because love heals. So you establish a momentum. Only when you reach agape, which is total love, are you impervious to wounds. This is the great goal for all.

We do not discount the need to receive love from others— loving intercourse is essential. Where you lack this, you deeply sense the void. However, for an adult, receiving expressions of loving intent from others is not primary; experiencing your own core of love comes first. Then you have a basis for relating maturely to another's core of love. You may keenly feel what you did not receive or what you are not receiving now. But if filling this need outside yourself is your focus, you will have a hard time filling it to your satisfaction.

There are not many people who have a strong connection with their own core of love. Therefore, there are not many who have that to give. Most people are hungry for love, even if they do not know it, and are looking to others for it. Where is it going to come from? Each person must find it in himself. Then it is available for others.

When you have a firm connection with your own core of love, you find that you have an infinite supply of it. What also happens is that everything in you that is not of love lines up at the water fountain to have a drink, so to speak. Your lack of loving intent surfaces where you had not been conscious of it before. This gives you an opportunity to further expand your core of love.

Love is the source of psychological healing as well as other levels of healing. Those who have no connection with their core of love can go to therapists for years and not heal, because only love understands. Learning to express anger and other negative feelings is healing to the extent that you are motivated by love. It may seem contradictory that you could be motivated by love to express rage, for example, but in fact love motivates you to meet and heal the unloving parts of yourself. You are not glorifying or empowering them, but bringing them into the light and releasing them in a harmless way.

I feel moved to complete with people in my life that I don't love, like my ex-husband, because agape is so important.

Although it is valuable to complete with people in your life, you can do so only when you are ready. If you do not yet love your ex-husband, it is because you do not yet know and understand him and what you experienced with him. When you are ready to, you will. It is all right to have your negative feelings as long as you need to. A cocoon becomes a butterfly when it is ready; all you can do is provide a safe place for it.

Someone who says he loves everybody may not yet be aware of negative feelings still in him. That is all right too; it is worthwhile to take an attitude of goodwill toward others. Wherever you are is your perfect starting point. You will not learn everything there is to know about loving by the last day of your last lifetime. It is an unending process.

Loving is not pasting on a smile and doing your version of good things for other people, whether you like it or not. That does not bring happiness or fulfillment. Loving must be genuine. You cannot force what is genuine. You can only nurture your process of opening to it. Love is delicate, yet infinitely strong. Once you open to your core of love, it makes itself known to you; it teaches you its ways. If you make demands on it, your connection with your core of love dims.

It takes attention to stay with your present experience of love. People often prefer to memorize rules instead. This is what religions tend to be about: "You do not have to be connected with your core of love. Just do what we say, and you will know what love is." However, there is no substitute for your core of love. When you are clearly connected to it, you are able to love in your own natural way. ❦

Part 4

FAMILY

RELATIONSHIPS

[Mostly to Specific Individuals]

❧ Chapter 16 ❧

PARENTS

START WITHIN

If you want a relationship with your parents and siblings, you can have one, but you must create it, starting from within. In your consciousness, allow each of them to love you as you are. See yourself as worthy of that love. Then love each of them as they are, and see them as worthy.

Focus on them one at a time and write down every reason you can think of why they should not love you. Then destroy that piece of paper. Do this daily until you cannot think of any reasons. Do the same for every reason you should not love them.

GET THE BALL ROLLING

My parents have difficulty expressing love. I have trouble feeling loved by them as a result. Do you have any suggestions?

Probably their own parents did not express much love to them, so they do not know what expressing love is like. It is never too late to learn. No doubt on some level, they long to freely express and receive love. Perhaps you could get the ball rolling by expressing love to them.

Think about expressions of love from them that you may have overlooked because they were nonverbal or less obvious. Acknowledge and express gratitude for them in writing, perhaps on the occasion of a holiday or birthday. Most people like to be acknowledged by others. This could open the door for greater sharing.

You may first need to deal with anger and hurt for what they did not give you. Otherwise these may block genuine recognition of and appreciation for what they did give you.

FATHER

To you, father represents power and, ultimately, God. You are still emotionally trying to appease an unanswering god. As long as you do this, you do not truly possess your own divinity and the personal power to create your world.

MOTHER

We suggest that you write a brief biography of your mother from what you know, describing her as accurately as you can. The more you describe her, the more you will know what is her and not you.

My mother passed away when I was two, and I would like to resolve my feelings about that so I can have cleaner and more appropriate relationships with women.

If you talk to your mother in your thoughts or write her a letter, she will hear and answer you, although you may not be aware of her responses at the time. You can work with her in fundamentally the same way as you would work with someone on the physical plane, even though your communication is obviously less concrete.

You no doubt felt angry as well as hurt about her leaving you. Often people are hesitant to acknowledge anger at someone who has died. It seems disrespectful, and there is fear that their anger may have somehow contributed to the person's death. But all your feelings have reasons, and they are there whether you acknowledge them or not. It is all right to be angry at your mother, and she certainly does not mind now.

You may be afraid to express anger toward women for fear that they, too, will abandon you. All you have to give women is who you are, and if at the moment that includes being angry, give them that in an appropriate way.

The best place to complete working out your feelings about your mother is in your current relationships with women, sexual or not. Your feelings are all there. Observe your patterns. From there you can start to rebuild your understanding of what women are and what you are in relationship to them.

RECEIVING LOVE FROM PARENTS

If you bring a belief from past lifetimes into this one that you are not loved, you may not be equipped to perceive the love your parents give you, especially if they are not demonstrative about it. You may also create an experience of actually being unloved. Either situation, as painful as it is, can help you recognize and change your belief.

If you choose parents who express love to you generously and obviously, and you do not change your belief, their behavior will not make sense to you. You might therefore rationalize that people act like they love you, but they really do not. This can further entrench your belief, because no expression of love from others will change your mind. Eventually you will probably push away others' love, because it does not conform to your belief.

By choosing parents who accurately reflect your belief by appearing not to love you, you might be in a better position to recognize and change your belief. This may not look like a positive experience at the time, but in the larger picture it could be a blessing. When you change your belief, you may begin to see love coming abundantly from many directions.

On the other hand, having parents who give you much love can help you change your belief, if you are willing. The main point is that whatever childhood you had, it can help you grow if you take advantage of it now. 🐚

Chapter 17

CHILDREN

TO SOMEONE TRYING TO GET PREGNANT

Your wish to have a child is valid and appropriate, but total acceptance of your present childlessness will make it easier for you to have one.

The body has the urge to parent so that the human race can survive. This urge is an important part of your biology, but people tend to unconsciously interpret it as a basic survival need. Obviously, it no longer is—in fact, survival is threatened by human overpopulation. However, when this urge is not fulfilled, people tend to be anxious. It might be useful to simply reassure yourself that you can relax because the human race will survive whether or not you have a child.

You have cultural pressures as well as biological urges. Perhaps other people question you about having children, or you compare yourself with couples who have children. Maybe your parents want to have grandchildren through you.

Rather than thinking of this as a time of waiting for a child, think of it as preparation. You can study different philosophies of child-rearing, and further develop your relationship with your mate. The longer you wait to have a child, the better parents you will be because of all the new things you are learning, and because of your growth in general.

Meanwhile, do things you enjoy that you will not be able to do easily once you are parents. If you have wanted to take a particular trip, for example, that would be encumbered by having a baby, do it now, if you can. Take advantage of the situation as it is.

You are having more lessons from not having a child right now than from having one. When you do not care that much one way or the other, you will probably become pregnant. Whatever time it takes for you both to get to that point will be your necessary preparation.

A CHILD'S LOVE

Infants, being wholly dependent, also provide acceptance and affection when their needs are met. Some people feel that through a child, they will at last have someone who accepts them completely. This motivation, though, is likely to lead to trouble. A child's love is marvelous, but seeing him as your source of love places a burden on him. When you are at your source, your child is free to simply be himself.

CHOOSING NOT TO HAVE CHILDREN

I'm 40 and I've mostly decided not to have children. My mother says to me, "There's no love like the love you have for your own child." Do you feel that it would be a great loss not to have a child?

When you say yes to one opportunity, you are saying no to others. Your soul seeks variety for increased learning, so different lifetimes have different themes. Your present lifetime is probably not about having children. You can trust your sensings in this regard. Love can be experienced in any circumstance.

It is true that there is no bond like that between mother and child. You have had that experience in many lifetimes. You can access it any time you wish. You might also like to have children in your life in a secondary way, such as through volunteering at a school or offering to baby-sit for a friend. That amount of contact with children may fully satisfy your needs without keeping you from filling other needs.

CHILDREN AND DIVORCE

About half of all marriages in the U.S. end in divorce. The odds are not in favor of someone avoiding that experience in this culture. Although divorce is difficult for children, it is not necessarily preferable for them to be in a situation in which their parents are together but are not getting along. Most children are strong and can recover from the stress of divorce if their parents are thoughtful of their needs.

Because of the publicity about the effects of parents on children, many parents are paralyzed with fear that they are going to ruin their children. The ones who are most concerned about this are the ones who are least likely to do so. It is those who are unconscious of their effects on their children who do the most damage. A person who cares about having a positive effect, although he is not going to do everything right, communicates that concern to his children, and that has a significant influence.

CARING FOR CHILDREN

There is nothing more important for children than the quality of energy they are given by their parents.

Children blossom the most when they are given the opportunity to make choices. We are not speaking of raising children without guidance or of "spoiling" them, but of allowing them the choices that they naturally gravitate toward whenever possible and appropriate.

Children will let you know if they have either too much or too little freedom, and it varies from child to child. Some children need a great deal of structure; some need relatively little. The more strong-willed the child, the more structure he generally needs. Some cultures promote a more structured approach to child-rearing than others. Ideally, however, parents can transcend cultural imprinting to discern the individual needs of their children.

Children see things quite differently than those who are older. Children focus on the immediate world. They are really not supposed to be concerned about long-term ramifications. That is part of their delight, that they have such a capacity to live in the present moment. They teach that to their elders, who, being more concerned with the long-term and the large picture, sometimes lose the intensity of the present moment.

Children require much from those around them. They cannot always give back what they are given. However, they will likely grow up themselves and give what you have given them to their children. So the circle continues.

Little should be demanded of children. Demands placed upon them tend to inhibit their growth. It is better to give them plenty of room to grow, to find their way. Of course, adults can and should provide guidance, but not too much; both too little and too much can be harmful. Most adults want to overly regiment children. Children have an inherent sensitivity to what they need in order to grow and develop. Adults can participate by giving them the wherewithal to follow their intuition.

The problem for many parent figures is that their own parents did not teach them how to be appropriate parents. In fact, anyone who tries to raise his children the way he was raised will probably not do as good a job as he will if he looks at parenting in a new way.

Most parenting styles treat children with little respect. If parents realize that their child's soul has likely had many lifetimes of development, and that it is only his body and personality that are less developed, there is a better basis for relationship.

We are not implying that children should be permitted to do anything they want to do. It takes a wise parent to perceive what guidelines are in the best interest not only of the child but all concerned. Guidelines for children should generally be simple, easily understood, consistent with one another, consistently enforced, and created in collaboration with the child, so that they work for the child as well as for the adults.

Let's make an analogy. Sometimes parents buy shoes for their children that are too big because the children will grow into them. But children are not comfortable in shoes that are too big. This is like not giving children enough guidance. They feel that they are adrift in too unstructured a space. On the other hand, some parents make their children wear old shoes that are too small because they do not wish to buy them bigger ones. In this case, their feet are cramped and cannot grow freely according to their own natural structure. This is like giving too much or the wrong kind of guidance.

Children should be addressed with the same respect that you would like to be addressed with, or more. They tend to live up to the way they are treated. If you treat a child as a fine, worthwhile, intelligent, and noble individual, he will tend to act like it. If, on the other hand, you treat a child as a terrible misbehaver, he tends to grow into that image.

As an adult, you have great responsibility because children look to adults to tell them what is what—children assume that you know. It is not always easy to respond appropriately when children press your buttons. As mentioned, children can be demanding, since they cannot fulfill many of their own needs. When your buttons are pushed, it is all right to acknowledge to yourself that you are irritated, angry, or whatever. However, before you say something to the child, it is wise to pause for a moment and see if what you are thinking about saying would actually help the situation. Later, you might also ask yourself why you were triggered. You may learn that it had relatively little to do with the child and more to do with something in you that is seeking healing. You can truly thank anyone who triggers you, because by being triggered you have an opportunity to heal that part of yourself so that you will not be triggered in that way again. The goal is to live by simply choosing appropriate actions without being triggered. Very few people are capable of this all the time, but it is a good goal to work toward. All relationships, including those with children, give you opportunities to practice this.

When children are acting inappropriately and need to be corrected, there are several possible approaches. One is to use your sense of humor to help them see what they are doing. By using humor, you can lighten the situation, taking some of the charge out of it. You can also question rather than accuse. You could say, for example, "Do you feel that you acted or spoke in the best way?" If the answer is no, you can then ask, "What might you have done differently?" That way you are on the child's side, helping him learn, rather than putting yourself in an adversarial relationship. There are times when an adversarial relationship is needed, but not often. Some children occasionally require you to use a great deal of emphasis in order to get through to them, while others never require more than a word or two. In any case, if you have developed good rapport with a child, it is easier to get through to him.

When your child misbehaves, discuss what the consequences should be, either now, or if he does it again. If he does not agree with you, find out why. If children know that you are being fair with them, they will usually be fair with you. Negotiate an agreement you can both live with. He is less likely to misbehave again if he has participated in determining the consequences, but if he does again misbehave, administer your agreement. In this way, he sees that he helped create his consequences, and will be less likely to grow up feeling like a victim of the world. He will also know that certain behaviors are not appropriate and will not be accepted.

It is important to understand the limits of a child's consciousness. A child, at least until about the age of ten or eleven, cannot really understand what you experience. He no doubt cares about you, but even that is partly out of natural self-involvement; a child cares about those who care for him. His job, if you want to call it that, is to survive and grow up; it is not really to look out for others. Many times, children do not want to share their toys. Although sharing can be encouraged in nonthreatening ways, a child who is afraid to share probably does not have much sense of security that his territory is safe. He clings to the things in it because his survival seems threatened.

Children grow and develop through their playing. Did you ever see a child who does not like to draw and color? Every child is attracted to such activities because they help him develop eye-hand coordination. It is not frivolous for children to draw. It helps them gain basic skills. In fact, all of a child's natural impulses are geared toward his later success in life.

There are reasons for every impulse in a child. Yes, children need to be contained sometimes. A child may want to gallop around the house while someone is sleeping. Rather than not letting him do it at all, it is preferable either to find another place where he can do it, or to agree on a later time when he can do it.

Children represent the child part of adults. Therefore, being with a child tends to awaken what has not been healed from your childhood, especially from when you were his specific age. That gives you much opportunity for healing. The essence of childhood is play. The child part of you, just like the child part of everyone else, longs to play, be free, have fun, be silly, make up games, and so forth.

This culture teaches that when you grow up, you eliminate the child part of yourself. But what in fact should happen is that you add adulthood to childhood, so you have both a child and adult part of you. Most adults lose the innocence and freedom of their child selves. They then spend the rest of their lives trying to compensate for that loss. It can be gratifying for adults to do art projects, dance, and so on, with children, pretending to be their age, at least a little. Every adult can use some of this. People who try to be adult all the time can easily lose joy.

A child's world, because it is one of exploration and experimentation, cannot be too structured. There are reasonable rules that can be enforced, but a child should not be expected to live in an overly structured environment. Again, this is not about permissiveness, which is a state in which adults are lazy and are not really there for their children. Obviously, there needs to be some structure—there is balance in all things. This balance is not always easy to find, but it is worth working toward.

MORE LISTENING

Both my children have attitude and emotional problems. What can I do to handle them?

One helpful approach would be an increase of listening, not only to what they say, but to what they do not say. Let them know that you are interested in their thoughts and feelings. Take the role of a reporter gathering information, staying neutral and objective. Do not immediately try to fix things. Part of their behavior likely stems from a lack of feeling heard, not just by you, and probably not just from this lifetime, although it surely relates to this lifetime. Listening of itself can be remarkably healing. In addition, when you deeply hear them, you will be much further along in knowing how you can make positive changes in their situation. ⚘

Part 5

MATE RELATIONSHIPS

❧ Chapter 18 ❧

FINDING YOUR MATE AND DEVELOPING INTIMACY

[A reminder: For simplicity, the pronouns he *and* him *generically refer to both men and women.]*

Finding a mate and developing intimacy are natural processes. They are not automatic; they do not happen without your participation, but the kind of participation that is effective is more akin to dancing than to conducting a military campaign. Some people in search of a mate go to great lengths to find one, organizing their lives around that quest. Participating in activities that interest you does help you meet those who share similar interests. However, if your primary purpose in doing so is to find a mate, you tend to work against yourself. For one thing, you are likely to put pressure on others in whom you have an interest, and this will tend to make them pull away from you.

Finding a mate is a by-product of living the life you most want to live in the way you most want to live it. If you are enjoying yourself, you are attractive to others who are enjoying themselves in similar ways.

What are you seeking in a mate, if you do not have one and would like one? You might be seeking intimacy, to see and be seen, to know and be known. Many people do not want intimacy. If you perceive that a potential partner does not want intimacy, and you do, you are wise to cross him off your list. There is no point in trying to change him so that he will want intimacy. You will probably not be successful. Besides, it is not loving or accepting to demand that someone change how he is to be your mate. If you truly love someone, you release him to be who he is. You do not require him to conform to your mold. Yet, loving yourself, you do not require yourself to give up something that is important to you in a relationship. So you let your connection with him be what it is—not intimate, not your primary relationship, but perhaps friendly, fun, and even an important part of your life.

Sometimes it is hard to give up relationships that are not working or potential relationships that clearly will not work. One reason might be the attitude that everything good is quite scarce, including potential mates. Your experience may seem to back up this view: you have been looking for the right person for many years, and he still has not arrived. It is true that the more specific your requirements, the longer it can take to find that person. But usually the key factor is not a scarcity of potential mates but your relationship with yourself. We are not implying that if you do not presently have a mate and you want one, there is something wrong with you. On the contrary, not having a mate might imply that you are engaged in an important inner process that you might not be able to engage in if you were mated. In any case, if you are not in a relationship, you have a special opportunity to be in a fulfilling relationship with yourself. The more you enjoy being with yourself and the less desperate you are for a mate, the more attractive you are. You can cultivate your relationship with yourself by doing things alone that you would like to do with a partner, such as going out or having a special evening at home, not waiting for someone else.

You do not need to become more attractive to have a mate. You are already attractive to prospective mates who complement you. Attractiveness is not an issue. However, if you have a belief that you are unattractive, you may want to change it, because it can cause you to get in your own way and suppress your natural attractiveness, making it harder for potential mates to see you and recognize how attractive you already are.

If you think that you have to change in order to find a mate, or even to be worthy of having a mate, you probably got that idea in your childhood. You may have felt that your parents did not love you fully, and that perhaps you could have convinced them to love you more if you had changed—if you had become better behaved, prettier, or more handsome. It is easy to understand why a child might get this kind of idea, but it is not an accurate perception.

You chose your genetic makeup and life situations, including your parents, not because there were no better ones around, or because you were inferior and did not deserve better, but because they were right for what you wanted to do in this lifetime. If your parents did not love you fully, you probably wanted to handle the lessons that situation tends to bring up.

When two people fit in a mate relationship, there is a multiplication of energy. You are both energized to do what you have come on earth to do. Of course, you feel this multiplication of energy whenever sex is fulfilling, and it is generally more fulfilling between two people who fit, in terms of what they have come to do.

The fitting mate for you is someone who wants to do something in his life that fits with what you want to do in your life. That is logical, isn't it? Sometimes mates are called partners. There must be something to partner; the partners must fit. If you were a ballroom dancer, you would not have an effective dance partnership with someone doing ballet. He might be good-looking and have a nice smile. You might even love him deeply. But if you decided to be partners and tried to dance, you would step on each other's toes. You would want swing music, and he would want Tchaikovsky—you would not get along in that situation. You might fit together as friends, or in working together in some other way, but not as dance partners.

Of course, you seek someone you deeply love and who loves you deeply; this is, obviously, essential between life mates. But love is not the only factor. In your development as a soul, you will ultimately learn to love in a way that includes everything. Even now, you probably love many people. Romantic love really is not all that different from any other type of love—at least in essence. Love is love. Love in a personal sense might be defined as caring deeply for another in such a way that a current of your energy moves to him. If you love someone, you are willing to share some of your being with him. In a romantic partnering, you obviously share your physical being; you have sex with one another. Sex can allow for intimacy on all levels—emotional, intellectual, and spiritual as well as physical. But everything you do can be an expression of love and a vehicle for intimacy. In a successful relationship, you mate with someone you love primarily because it works for you to do so.

When looking at potential mates, you are wise to be clear-eyed about what is workable. You do not serve yourself by disregarding this. If you meet someone who is the apparently right age, gender, and size, in the "right" career, and so forth, do not assume that this implies that you have found your mate. You may well have made some agreements on an essence level, but they may not have been to mate; mating may not be very workable. On the other hand, someone who is in the "wrong" package might make a splendid mate for you. We are not attempting to give you parameters, but to help you see beneath the surface. Look for what you really share.

Many things must click into place for a mate relationship to work. Your rhythms need to be aligned, or be capable of aligning. The longer you know someone, the easier this is. If you knew someone in past lives and developed a rapport, it makes it easier to be together as mates in this lifetime, even if your past experience together was not as mates. However, no matter how much time you spent together in past lives, you still need to get to know one another in this lifetime.

The term "soul mate" can have different meanings, but many people define it as one soul with whom you want to mate in all your lifetimes. Actually, your soul wants a variety of experiences. You can only gaze into someone's eyes for so many centuries!—then you need to get on with other things. We advise against waiting around for your soul mate to come.

Most people have what we have termed an *essence twin*, also known as a *twin soul*. This is the soul with whom you are closest. It might be described as your learning partner for this planet. You have many kinds of relationships together, including parent/child, sibling, and friendship; you are mated in relatively few of your lifetimes. You also choose not to be together in a substantial number of lifetimes. Some people are referring to the essence twin when they use the term *soul mate.* There are other souls with whom you have mated several times in the past. Therefore, after all you have learned, you get along well and like being together. If you have agreed to possibly mate again in this lifetime, you might also be called "soul mates," especially if mating again is a high priority. Incidentally, you might be surprised at how many people in your life you have known in past lifetimes. That includes people you work with as well as your friends.

When you are planning your upcoming lifetime before you incarnate, you usually find some of your old friends who are also planning to incarnate in the same general vicinity. You might say to one of them something like, "I enjoyed being your mother in ancient Rome. Why don't we try getting together as partners in this lifetime?" If your life plans fit together reasonably well, he might reply, "That sounds good to me; I do have nine other mate agreements, but I will put you on my list. If we run into each other and it feels right at the time, let's do it." He probably will not mate with all ten possibilities on his list, at least not for very long. However, these mate agreements, along with the other agreements he has made, give him a strong yet flexible foundation for his life.

There are many unpredictable factors on the physical plane. You or those with whom you made mate agreements might have ended up in unexpected locations or situations, and might have gotten involved with other people. This is why you make so many mate agreements.

You have probably already met people with whom you have mate agreements, perhaps in high school or college. You might have gone out together, even recently. You usually feel connected to them, but mate relationships with them do not necessarily turn out to be workable or even compatible. Because of free choice, your souls cannot fully predict how you will develop as people or what your reaction will be to one another "in the flesh." The unpredictability of life is part of the game; it is not "bad." In any case, you generally seek out those on your list before looking seriously at other possibilities, and will probably cross names off it as you go through life. If you meet everyone on your list that you are going to meet, and none of them prove appropriate, you might start going through your "backup" list, or you might simply open yourself to other friends, old and new.

When you made your mate agreements before your lifetime, you were not all-wise and all-knowing. You did not think of everyone who might have made an appropriate mate, nor did you know what the future would bring. There is nothing wrong with choosing someone not on your list as your partner. However, those on your list generally fit from one important standpoint: what they wish to accomplish in their lives is compatible with what you wish to accomplish in yours. On the other hand, many people never do what they set out to do, usually because of false personality [*see Glossary*]. Your compatibility in terms of life task can be insignificant in a relationship with someone who is not interested in doing what he came to do. But if you both are interested in completing your life tasks, this can aid your relationship a great deal. Compatibility of life tasks can also be present when there is no mate agreement, although, of course, that is not certain.

Your soul and spirit guides are constantly working to bring you together with others with whom you have agreements, mate and otherwise. You do not always meet those you plan to, but you often do. Particularly when you sleep, your soul and those of the people with whom you have agreements plan how you might meet. When you are awake, your guides coach you to be where those people are, and those people's guides coach them to be where you are. Of course, people often do not follow their guidance, so it may take several tries. The closer you come to one another, the more strongly you attract each other. To make an analogy, your agreements are like magnets that are electrically boosted by your soul when you are in the vicinity of those with whom you have the agreements.

Since your soul and spirit guides are already working with you to help you meet those with whom you have agreements, how can you help the process along? For one thing, be alert to intuitive "flashes" and be willing to follow them. If you get a strong feeling that you should go somewhere, or take a different route than you usually take, you might want to pay close attention. It may indicate that you are trying to keep a date. You may feel foolish sometimes; you may say to yourself, "I don't know why I am going to the mall. I don't need anything," yet you go, and you meet someone you would not have met otherwise. This is not necessarily someone with whom you have a mate agreement, but he may introduce you to a person with whom you have a mate agreement, or he may enhance your life in some other way.

When you are learning to perceive intuitively, there are times when, for example, you go to the mall and nothing happens. It may be that you did have a "date" with someone important to you, and at the last minute something came up for him, or you just missed one another. There is no need to fret when this occurs. You usually get many more opportunities to meet. If you had only one chance to meet the important people in your life, you seldom would. It is also possible that what you thought was intuition was your subconscious mind sending you an impulse because a part of you wanted to buy something new, or some such thing. It takes work to learn to perceive impulses accurately.

Another thing you can do is connect with those with whom you have mate agreements in your consciousness through meditation. It is especially successful late at night or early in the morning when they are likely to be sleeping, unless you happen to catch them meditating at the same time. You can connect with another person at any time, but if he is busy in an outer sense, less of him is available to connect with you. To make the connection, simply go into a deeply relaxed state and ask to be connected with the person with whom you have a mate agreement whom you are most likely to meet next. During the first meditation, it is a good idea to simply feel his energy. This will aid you in identifying him if and when you finally do meet. This will also give him a chance to tune in to your energy as a human being. In subsequent meditations, you can communicate, discussing your life in your mind's eye. You can, for example, tell him the location where you work, and that you are a Mets fan and can often be found at Shea Stadium, for instance; it does not hurt to name specific dates. On a conscious level, he is not going to retain these facts, but there will probably be some penetration, and you increase your chances of meeting. When you are done, do not worry about what happens; let it go.

Rather than focusing on connecting with one specific person, you can also ask in meditation to be connected with all the people with whom you have mate agreements, or with everyone who might be an appropriate mate. In communicating with them, tell them who you are, what you are looking for, and where you can be found. It is rather like putting out a personal ad into the universe on a radio signal saying that you are here and available.

Affirmations can be helpful. Your thinking magnetizes people who have complementary thinking. If you change your thinking, you can change what and whom you magnetize. One basic affirmation you could use in finding a mate is:

> I am now attracting to myself a mate who is a joy to
> be with, and to whom I bring joy.

That covers a lot of ground, doesn't it? If you find it a joy to be together, many things are working properly. You do not have to specify, "I am now attracting to me someone who has blonde hair, green eyes, and is five-foot-six to five-foot-eight," because if those qualities are the only ones that will truly bring you joy in a mate relationship, you will attract them. (Of course, you might be surprised.)

There is a prevalent expectation that when you meet the "right" person, you will be metaphorically struck by lightning. You will see him, preferably across a crowded room, and, as if by magic, you will walk toward one another and fall into a passionate embrace. We are exaggerating a little bit, but not much. You may expect that when you meet the right person, you will know immediately. Sometimes that happens, especially if it is someone with whom you have deep and long-standing connections from past lifetimes. Often, however, "love at first sight" is more indicative of strong physical attraction than it is of "fate." If you prematurely decide that someone is "the one" and start placing expectations on a relationship too quickly, you are likely to twist or even ruin it.

Many relationships that work begin gently. Often you do not know when you first meet someone what is possible between you, and that can be an advantage. The first part of building a workable relationship is friendship. This provides the foundation for what is to come. You may feel comfortable with someone but not think of him as mate material at first. Sometimes you may even dislike him, perhaps because of unpleasant past lifetimes together, or people of whom he reminds you. Nevertheless, in time your relationship may grow.

Desperation is not a strong foundation for a long-lasting relationship. If you have been without a good relationship for a long time, you may have a certain amount of tension or even panic. The longer it has been, the more tension you are likely to have. Part of this may stem from sexual frustration. Using masturbation to at least somewhat fulfill your own sexual needs can be helpful. It can also help you practice loving yourself.

No one "must" have a relationship with someone else. Relationships are potentially lovely and growthful experiences, but you will not die if you do not have one, and there are many other pleasures in life. If you have a lot of charge around this issue, your first step in having the relationship you want is to not want it so much. Relaxing your grip will allow new things to begin to happen.

When you emphasize in your mind how much you want a relationship and how frustrated you are at not having one, you put out a counterproductive energy. It is like repeating a negative affirmation that states, "I don't have a relationship. I can't have one," making it more likely that you will not. It is similar to trying to get your car out of the snow; if the wheels spin, you get more stuck. You have to put something under the wheels to give them traction and move the car ahead. A new belief that relationships are enjoyable, easy, and fun to be in is the traction that moves you ahead into that experience.

The degree to which you are desperate to have a relationship is often the degree to which another part of you does not want one. You may have fears of which you are not even conscious. A relationship may suggest imprisonment to you, a lack of being able to do the things you want to do. If you can bring these fears to the surface and examine them, you can make choices about them. You can say, "Well, yes, I would give up some things, but I would get other things. I can accept some compromise and still make sure that I have the freedom I need."

Once you are in a relationship, how can you develop intimacy? One key is honesty. Some people tell little lies about themselves when they first begin a relationship. This is destructive to intimacy, because your partner will never be completely sure if you are telling the truth. It is much easier to maintain credibility if you start out being credible. This is not to say that you must talk about things you are not ready to talk about, but neither do you have to falsify information. There are times when lying is appropriate, but rarely with someone with whom you wish to have intimacy. Even lying about your age says to the other person, "There is something about me I do not want you to know. This is the boundary of our intimacy." If you want to be known and understood, you must make yourself knowable and understandable.

Communication needs to be not only honest, but clear and complete. Communicating with another person—any person, not only your mate—is a challenge, because each person speaks a slightly different language, with different assumptions and definitions. You must be deliberate and alert to make yourself clear to others. It is not a bad idea for couples to put their fundamental agreements in writing and refine them over time, so that they are clear. The refinement process can also help each partner become more aware of what he is feeling.

People often have the unrealistic notion that if somebody really loves you, he knows all you want, need, or mean without your having to clarify it. Since human beings are generally not telepathic, this does not usually occur. If you take responsibility for communicating what you want, need, and mean, you avoid unnecessary disappointments and misunderstandings. Misunderstandings destroy intimacy more than any other factor, and most of them can be avoided. Of course, the more deeply someone knows you, the more aware he is of your wants and needs, and of how you communicate. Nonetheless, as you change and grow, it is important to stay up to date with each other.

Intimacy needs space and time to grow. If two people have packed schedules day in and day out, they probably do not share much intimacy. Intimacy implies being with the other person, being there in the present, in both conversation and silence. It may include expressing difficult emotions; a clear and appropriate expression of anger, for example, can bring two people closer together. Any time you love someone enough to tell him how you feel, you are offering a bridge that can enable him to know you better. Of course, bridges go both ways—you can get to know him better as well.

You cannot be any more intimate with another person than you are with yourself. How can you expect someone else to know what you are feeling, for example, when you yourself do not know what you are feeling? You can develop intimacy with yourself in the same ways that work with others: be honest with yourself, communicate clearly with yourself, and give yourself space and time to be with yourself.

You cannot expect any other person—even someone who conforms to your fantasies in every detail—to give you what you feel is missing within you. You must do that yourself. If, for instance, you lack a sense of self-worth, you are likely to attract a partner who mirrors your view of yourself, who treats you as if you were worthless. Why? Because it is confusing when a partner insists that you are worthy when you are certain that you are not, and people do not like to be confused. If you are fortunate enough to have a partner who tries to inspire a sense of self-worth in you, but you are not willing to accept it, you will probably deflect his input or dismiss him entirely. You might, for instance, tell yourself that he is prejudiced, or think, "What does he know?"

Anything you have not yet dealt with in yourself will likely come up at some point in the context of a mate relationship. Therefore, if you are single and have been making use of your time alone to release your old patterns, you will have an easier time when you form a relationship. However, no one is finished processing everything. The more you are willing to acknowledge and work on your shortcomings, without self-judgment, the easier it will be to develop intimacy with a partner. One reason is that you are less defensive.

Many fights arise over defensiveness. Suppose you are in a relationship with someone who says to you, "You are selfish about the television. We always have to watch what you want to watch." What would most people's response be? Probably an automatic "No, I'm not!" Suppose that, instead, you say, "Hmm...I wasn't conscious of that. Thank you for pointing that out." After giving it some thought, you discuss possible solutions, such as taking turns, or getting another television— you agree that you do not always have to watch together. Also, since you had not been aware of the problem, you ask him to be clearer in saying what he wants to watch. Because you were open rather than defensive, he does not have to be angry about that issue anymore. You have heard and received his complaint. If your partner complains about something you do not agree with, or are not able to do something about, your willingness to hear and discuss it can still help defuse the issue.

Some people want to get a relationship set up so that it is running smoothly and they never have to do anything about it again. However, this does not usually work. To make an analogy, someone may build his dream house and move into it;

however, he must continually refine and maintain it. In a sense, a house is never done. The same is true of relationships. They keep changing, providing opportunities for growth, as the people in them change and grow. There is nothing wrong with that. Wouldn't it be boring if you felt that you had everything set up, that you always knew what to expect from your partner? It is more fun to be constantly looking for the unexpected, discovering new things, and changing.

Sometimes relationships change to the point where they are no longer workable in that form. Maybe the form needs to be changed to a more distant relationship, a friendship perhaps. That is not necessarily an indication of anyone's failure; you may have simply completed your work together. Ending or changing a relationship gracefully, without making anyone wrong, is a mark of maturity. The more quickly you acknowledge that a relationship is no longer serving you, the sooner you can move on to your next step. That may be a relationship that does serve you, or a period of aloneness. Of course, some relationships are fitting and adaptable enough to serve you for the rest of your life.

How do you know whether to keep working on a relationship or to let it go? There are no hard and fast rules about this, but generally, if you have an automatic impulse to run, there is a good chance that you would benefit from staying with it. If you have an automatic impulse to hang onto it, it is likely that you would be well advised to let it go. The key factor is your motivation. If your impulse is to run, it is likely to be because of laziness, not wanting to do the necessary work, or fear of what that work might bring up. If your impulse is to hang onto the relationship, it is likely to be because of fear that you will not find anyone else, perhaps because you are not lovable enough. It is preferable to stay in a relationship because you genuinely want to.

If you have mixed feelings—part of you wants to stay with it, and part of you wants to leave it—it is helpful to evaluate how much energy it would take to get the relationship working well, if that is even possible. You may need the help of a professional counselor to clearly identify the relationship's problems and possible solutions. If it looks like it would require a lot of work to reap relatively little improvement in it, your highest growth might be found in letting go of the present relationship. That would reinforce a belief that you deserve to be well treated and have enriching relationships that come easily to you. On the other hand, you might realize that even if the chances of changing the relationship are relatively low, you would grow a great deal in some necessary skills by making the attempt. Of course, you might also discover that your relationship is fundamentally sound, and that relatively little effort could reap major improvements in it.

If you are in doubt, you might wish to have a trial separation, and see what you feel. Do you feel unfinished, that you still want to be together? Sometimes it helps to explore your feelings with an objective third party, but only you can know for yourself what is right for you. If you are willing to see the truth, what is right for you will usually become clear to you in time.

It is generally assumed that an ideal relationship lasts for the rest of your life, is monogamous, includes a house with a fence, perhaps two or three children, and so forth. That is not necessarily the case.

Monogamy is not the ideal for everyone. In fact, many marriages are not wholly monogamous, in spite of the often-unexamined rule that they should be. Sometimes this is due to a lack of maturity. Other times, one or both of the partners are not innately suited for monogamy, or may have important essence agreements to fulfill outside their primary relationship that involve sex. That is not necessarily a "bad thing." Monogamy is promoted in this society to provide stability. When people are mature, they may be capable of handling more complex arrangements without a loss of stability. Neither monogamy nor alternative forms of relationship are "good" or "bad," moral or immoral—it is a matter of choice, but alternative forms are usually more challenging.

Most people need some sort of structure and definition to their relationships. It can be rigid or flexible, but people ordinarily like to know where things stand. Group marriages and other more flexible arrangements will likely become more common in years to come. But however your relationship is set up, it is important for everyone concerned to be clear on what your agreements and boundaries are, especially if you wish to deviate from the norm. Otherwise, it will be difficult to maintain the relationship.

You have the right in your relationships to negotiate agreements that work for you as well as for your partner(s). You also have the right to renegotiate them if your needs change. If you are clear that you are not suited for monogamy, it is important to be honest about this with prospective partners. You may lose the relationship, but you prevent painful problems later for both of you. You might also find that your prospective partner feels the same way you do. Your honesty helps him be open about it too, and allows you to make specific agreements about how you are going to handle an open relationship. The majority of people prefer a one-on-one relationship and find it easiest. For one thing, it is not smart to bring more people into the picture if you have not yet learned how to be with one other person. But if you cannot live with long-term monogamy, those with whom you have mate agreements probably feel the same way. You do not have to fit yourself into a mold. You do not necessarily have to give up things you truly want and need in order to have other things you truly want and need. First, though, you must know what you want and need, what you must have in a relationship to be fulfilled.

If you were to list the things you need to have a fulfilling relationship, you might find the list to be long and maybe quite limiting. That is all right, if you truly need all of them. It is better to be clear on this from the beginning than to later find yourself feeling stuck in a relationship that is not fulfilling to you. However, as you explore what you need, you might find that some of your preconceptions no longer hold true for you.

It is easy to see this with your physical and professional ideals. Be open to many different physical types. We are not saying that you should get involved with someone to whom you are not attracted, but perhaps you can discover that you are attracted to many types of people. This, of course, gives you more potential mates. Also, if you have always thought that your ideal mate would be an artist, for example, maybe what you really desire is someone who has an artistic sensibility, including sensitivity and a love of beauty. There are, of course, people with these traits who are not artists.

Relationships are one of the most important areas of learning on the physical plane. Therefore, it is worthwhile to examine old assumptions and premises about them so that you can fully take advantage of the opportunities they provide. If you do not have a mate, having one will not solve all your problems; conversely, if you are in a mate relationship that is not satisfying, not having that relationship will not solve all your problems either.

Problems are your teachers. In finding their solutions, you do what you came here to do, which is to grow, expand, and become more capable of love. Love is who and what you are. As you function more and more effectively in the realm of relationships, more and more of who you are comes forth. The love comes through, not just because the other person is present, but because you are more present.

It seems that the people I'm strongly attracted to are never right, or don't respond.

There are many things to consider here. If you continually attract people who are not right for you, perhaps you need to develop in yourself a clearer understanding of what is right for you.

You might ask also yourself what they symbolize to you. Being attracted does not necessarily mean that you are being attracted to potential mates. There may be a quality in them that you want to have more of in yourself. Opposites do often attract. If, for example, you are easygoing, you might attract dynamic types of people because you want to learn to be more dynamic. If you practice being more dynamic, you may find that your attraction to them on that basis begins to fade.

I'm with someone right now with whom I'm very comfortable, but I'm wondering if we've hit some limitations we can't get beyond. Is it possible to be comfortable, yet still have to go on a different course?

Your feelings are a good gauge of what is going on. If you still feel good in the relationship, that it is serving you and that you are growing in it, then it probably still has value. It depends on how you experience comfort. If comfort for you is an avoidance of growth and meeting issues, then you may be in a rut. But there is certainly nothing wrong with being comfortable in a relationship. In fact, it might be evidence that it is working well.

It sounds as if you feel that something is missing for you. Give some thought to what that might be, and see if you can create it in your present relationship or in a platonic friendship. If not, decide if you are willing to let go of what you have in order to seek it. Every day you stay in a relationship, you are making a choice to do so. Knowing what motivates your choice helps you choose consciously.

My husband and I no longer wish to be with one another, but we have children and an obligation to look after his mother.

In solving problems, you grow and expand. Your problem here is how to meet your own needs as well as your commitments to others. When there are children involved, you do not necessarily serve them by staying together. If you are apart, it can require ingenuity to make sure that their needs continue to be met, but no doubt you can find ways to accomplish this. There may also be no reason why you could not continue to help care for your mother-in-law after the separation, if you choose to.

There is usually a way to solve a problem. You are not stuck. If you and your husband truly wish to be apart, you can probably work it out.

There are some people in my life who don't seem to have any real problems. They have excellent marriages, and everything goes all right, without complications. How do they get off so easily?

Each path in life is unique. Of course, you may not know what is really going on; you are only seeing part of the picture. But suppose that you are correct that they have excellent, smooth relationships. That may be what they chose for this life. You, on the other hand, may have chosen to deal with some important, challenging issues that require your undivided attention. Comparisons with other people in this regard are not valid; others have what they need to grow, and you have what you need. If your life could be different than it is, it would be. The fact that it is not fulfilling you in specific ways means that there are areas of growth available that will bring the fulfillment you seek.

I want to end my relationship, but my partner doesn't. Will I form karma with him if I leave him? Wouldn't unconditional love require that I stay with him?

You do not create karma unless you violate your partner. He does not have the right to keep you in a relationship you do not wish to be in, and vice versa. You would only create karma in such a situation if you abandoned a partner who had no other means of support, and it resulted in his harm or untimely death.

You can end a relationship in a loving manner. That involves finding out what your partner needs in order to feel complete and resolved, as well as doing what you need in order to feel complete and resolved. You might undertake some counseling together to have clear communication and a more graceful shift in your relationship. It is not necessarily loving to stay in a relationship that no longer serves you. If it no longer serves you, it probably does not actually serve him either, even if it is comfortable for him. If you are unhappy in the relationship, you are not likely to give unconditional love to it. On the other hand, there is no reason you cannot be unconditionally loving as you end the relationship.

The way you end a relationship is as important as the way you start it. It says more about you and your integrity than almost any other time in a relationship. At the beginning, if you want what your partner has to give, you may be on your better behavior or do things just to please him. That is not unconditional love. When you decide that you no longer want the relationship, you reveal your true colors. Your kindness, sensitivity, and appropriateness become especially significant. But being kind does not mean staying in a relationship that is stunting you. Being kind means communicating your experience in a way that is honest yet not unnecessarily hurtful. Being kind means taking his needs into account, so that you allow the transition to be fair and workable. You do not just leave; you end the relationship with grace and care. You balance your needs with his.

If you commit to a mate relationship with someone, presumably you love him, however you define love. If it is genuine love, your care and concern do not stop just because you no longer wish to be in that relationship. If you now feel that you do not love him in any way, you probably did not have a true or mature experience of love all along. In that case, some self-examination is warranted.

If your partner was irresponsible and uncaring both during a relationship and while ending it, how do you deal with that and break the attachment?

It is important to have support from others. Those who have gone through something similar can be especially helpful.

If someone is irresponsible and uncaring in a relationship, recognizing that you are fortunate to be free of him can aid you in breaking your attachment to him. Examining why you became attached to someone with those qualities to begin with can also be helpful. Learning to fill more of your own needs, meeting other people, and the simple passage of time can all assist you in the transition.

Could you suggest some techniques for dealing with unresolved feelings about a previous lover?

You might write him a series of letters pouring out all your feelings. Keep throwing them away until you find it natural to write a neutral, balanced letter. You may or may not want to mail that letter.

You also might examine what he represents to you, and why he is still on your mind. Changing something in your life now may help you release these feelings.

How does homosexuality fit into all this? Is it okay to go in that direction if you feel you want to?

The principles governing relationships and intimacy are the same regardless of sexual orientation. In fact, they apply not only to mate relationships but to other kinds as well.

There is nothing intrinsically wrong or right with either homosexuality or heterosexuality. It is a matter of what your path is. If you are in conflict over it, resolving that conflict is part of your life task and will bring you growth. Many people in such conflict are in fact bisexual, yet are blocked for one reason or another in the full and free expression of that bisexuality. Working to release that or any block can be beneficial.

MEDITATION

Imagine yourself in the ideal relationship. There is no need to try to picture the other person, and you can do this even if you are in a relationship now. See yourself as you would be in a partnership that works well. Feel how dynamic you are. Feel the flow moving between you and your partner. Feel the fun you are already having as an individual increasing by reason of having someone with whom to share it. Feel total connection moving out from you to him. Feel how much you like him. Feel how much you enjoy being in a healthy, satisfying relationship. Also, feel how much you enjoy being in relationship with yourself. Take a moment and let all this come together in you. The feelings are there; all you have to do is let them in. ⁅

WORKING WITH MATE RELATIONSHIPS
[Mostly To Specific Individuals][9]

ROOM IN YOUR LIFE

B oth neediness and false self-sufficiency stem from fear and are obstacles to attracting successful relationships. In false self-sufficiency, you take the defensive attitude that you do not need anyone else, and therefore you are not sufficiently open to receive a mate.

Neediness arises from believing that another person is going to take care of you and make you feel good about yourself. Neediness pushes away what is longed for, because under the neediness is belief in the lack of what you long for. Most people instinctively avoid those who are extremely needy, which can actually work to the benefit of the needy person. It highlights the neediness and encourages him to deal with it. If someone comes along who for some reason says, "I will fill your void," a rather unhealthy relationship is likely to develop. That, too, provides lessons for both. The void cannot truly be filled by someone else. You can only know oneness with others to the degree that you have an inner sense of wholeness to share.

In wholeness, your desire for a partnership comes from knowing that you would enjoy the possibilities it would bring to your life, and that you have room for it, without neediness.

COMING CLOSE

Sometimes you ask for things that part of you does not want. In asking for a romantic relationship, how truly willing are you to

---

[9]A reminder: The original channelings were spoken to both men and women. Again, for simplicity, the pronouns *he* and *him* have been used, in editing this book, to represent both male and female. When *he* is used, it should not be inferred that Michael was necessarily speaking to a woman about a man.

have it? Part of you may be effectively avoiding having one because of painful past experiences. Even if you consciously want a relationship, if part of you does not, you must deal with that before you can have what you are asking for.

I don't understand why people are afraid to be close.

Many people believe that closeness brings hurt.

ASKING THE UNIVERSE

Asking the universe for a mate does not mean that you then stop putting forth energy to create what you are looking for. Your part of the bargain is to do everything you can to help it happen, including putting yourself in circulation so that potential partners can find you.

AN ABUNDANCE OF RELATIONSHIPS

Rather than waiting for "the" person to appear, why don't you welcome an abundance of nurturing relationships? You do not yet know what sort of person is really for you, so by having experiences, you will be better equipped to know, and thereby create the "ideal" relationship. It is not wise to try to skip steps, because it leaves out valuable development.

MAKING CHOICES

Why do men always leave me?

Men do not leave you, in the sense you mean. Men, like women, simply make choices about what they want in their lives. That has less to do with you personally than you think. Interpreting this as desertion is due to your belief that men do not like you. You can change this belief.

When you are with a man who does not match your energy, the relationship has an imbalance. Eventually, that will likely be recognized by at least one of you. It takes a little experimenting to find the right match. If you have limited experience with men, you have no way of knowing whether you have really found it, because you do not have a basis of comparison.

Enjoy the process of dating. Have fun seeing what happens with different types of energies. The reason you rushed into your marriage was that you wanted to avoid the process of determining in yourself what is right for you. You had little confidence in your attractiveness to men and felt it was better to hold onto what appeared to be your best opportunity.

MARRIAGE

Marriage will not solve all your problems and make everything all right somehow. Prince Charming is here to work on himself just as surely as you are. Your marriage is a framework in which many of your unresolved issues can come up and be dealt with. It also gives you a partner for mutual support and fun—do not forget the fun!

FLEXIBILITY

You can afford to relax and trust. The primary trust is trust in yourself, trust that your own innate spiritual knowledge will guide you. Secondarily, you can trust your mate and the universe in which you both live. You can trust that you each have a desire, beneath whatever fears remain, to see and do the right thing. When you are loving, you call forth love in him. When you are reacting, you call forth reaction in him. Obviously, life is much gentler and easier when lived from love.

You can assume that you will each see things in different ways, that you will not agree on many details. You have much to learn in appropriately negotiating, being clear about the things you feel most strongly about, and being willing to be flexible on points that are not really that important to you. You need to prioritize, bend, and recognize that you have equal needs: one person's needs are not more important than the other's. Look for the truth, and seek a balanced and appropriate solution, rather than trying to make things come out to your personal greatest gain. It is sometimes hard to do that when you feel threatened, so you need to be a loving friend to yourself to help calm your inner upsets, which are certainly going to come up.

When you are controlled by fear, you tend to be overly attached to things being a certain way. That is a form of enslavement. The more flexible you are, the more freedom and joy you can have.

If your emphasis in a relationship, any kind of relationship, is on how you can best support the other person, your differences can be more or less easily resolved. When your emphasis is on changing the other person or gaining an upper hand, your differences are magnified.

PROJECTION

On the physical plane, you externalize your consciousness. Often that means that you project parts of yourself that you do not like onto other people. When you see the projection, you can learn more about these parts, and learn to accept, love, and heal them. Until you separate your projection from the reality of the person onto whom you are projecting, you cannot truly see and connect with him. Sometimes in the beginning of relationships, there is mutual recognition, before this projection takes over. You might also project of aspects of yourself that you like, which is more pleasant, but it is still not true recognition.

One who is aspiring to be a fully conscious human being needs to recognize this element of projection. A good way to do this is to simply ask yourself what part of you the other person represents. It can also be useful to observe the other person as a scientist might, with as much objectivity as possible. You may notice qualities that do not fit with the image you are projecting. This is especially easy if you observe him relating to other people, who may not be projecting the same things onto him.

A person who no longer needs to project onto others is, you might say, on the fast track of spiritual growth, but some people do need to learn in this slower, more painful way for a while.

FEAR

There is always fear when it comes to human relationships: fear that the other person will leave, or fear that he will not leave; fear that you will feel empty, or fear that you will be filled so full that you will lose yourself.

Recognize where fear is a motivation. Feel your fear fully. Know your fear. Do not bury it. Let it out so it can change into knowledge.

SETTING BOUNDARIES

As long as he knows that whatever he does, you will tolerate it because you so desperately need him, you are inviting him to continue in old patterns.

If you are finding it unpleasant to be in his presence, remove yourself from it. You have been less willing to do this than you might have been because your need for him is so great.

BEING MALE

Every man has a "macho" side. It is the personality that springs from the masculinity of the body. If a man denies that, he denies what would help him feel good in his body. On the other hand, if he is no more than that, he is little indeed. There is a balance.

You do not have to be the ideal man, just the man you are.

Many men think that love is a specialty of women. Since love is all there is, when you get right down to it, this indicates a misunderstanding of love. There is a female way of loving and a male way of loving. The male way of loving tends to be more focused and directional. The female way of loving tends to be more unfocused and encompassing; therefore, it feels softer. Both aspects of love are needed. It is also true that every person has both masculine and feminine ways of loving, although men usually emphasize the masculine way, and women, the feminine. The degree to which men honor the feminine way of loving as manifested through the women in their lives is the same degree to which they honor it in themselves. The reverse is true for women. Having access to both ways of loving gives you the ability to be soft as well as hard, gentle as well as firm, delicate as well as bold, and heartfelt as well as reasoned.

Each person has his own way of loving, his own unique combination of elements. The way you love is perfect for you. Do not be afraid to experience what love truly is for you. If you are afraid of it, you have not yet known it—it is your very nature. You being truly yourself is the greatest gift of love you can bring. There is no greater satisfaction than to love truly.

A LIGHT TOUCH

Virtually everyone goes through the fear of loss when he finds something he deems valuable, be it love, money, or position. The tendency is to hold on to it for dear life, not realizing that squeezing something will cause it to want to escape from your grasp. It is better to hold things lightly.

Our suggestion is to chill out, as they say. Here is a person whom you love very much. Love him enough to let him be. That will make him happiest, and will, incidentally, bring you more of the things you most desire. This is not to say that you should not express your feelings, but do it lightly and appropriately, in a way he can hear.

LETTING GO

We suggest that you lighten up. You are taking this process too seriously. In a "worst case" scenario, you would break up. That would not be the unmitigated disaster you feel it would be. Besides, nothing is final. Perhaps you need to break up and come back together later to most effectively realize the potential of your relationship. You have so many preconceptions about all this. Let them go, and you will be much happier in the relationship.

You tend to see this relationship as being central in your life. It is not. Your relationship with yourself is central. Whether or not you have a relationship with any other person, you will always have your relationship with yourself. Be happy in that love affair.

If you are fully prepared to be alone again, you decrease the chances of that being necessary. Aloneness can have great value. It is not the torture you fear it would be, although we do not underestimate the pleasures of true partnership. That, however, takes two, and if a partner is not available, it is not the end of the world.

The more you keep your sense of humor and perspective, the better things will go with others.

BALANCE

Sometimes, to find balance, you have to go to the opposite extreme for a while. Suppose that you have been in a relationship that is intense and hot but based on neediness. You decide that you are getting "singed" too much. You go to the other extreme and get involved in a relationship that is familiar, repetitive, and based on comfort. That becomes uninvolving. You then deliberately plant yourself in the middle and bring in what was exciting in the first relationship, without the neediness, and what was calm in the second, without the repetitiveness.

In a way, this is the pattern of all growth: you go from one extreme to the other and finally find the center. There are things to learn from both extremes, so it is not a waste of effort.

If you love someone intensely because you need him a great deal, the intensity of your love amplifies your neediness and throws you more out of balance. If, after some growth, you go to the other extreme and decide that you do not need him at all, your love may diminish. In balance, you can have love without neediness that can grow in intensity indefinitely without destructiveness. It is like building a fire: if you do it properly, you can make it bigger and more intense without it getting out of control.

However, once you eliminate neediness, other distorting factors can come up to be dealt with. You have to keep processing out impurities to keep your love in balance.

ENDING A RELATIONSHIP

I can't decide whether to end the relationship I'm in. I feel tied to him, but I also feel a need to move on. I feel trapped, because if I do move on, I'll feel responsible for him, and I worry that I may be making the biggest mistake of my life.

If you are having such thoughts, you are not finished with the relationship. Obviously, there are things in it that are not satisfactory for you. Look at how you have participated in creating an unsatisfactory relationship. See how you can avoid those pitfalls in the future.

You are not responsible for another independent human being. You may have allowed him to become dependent upon you in certain ways. Whether or not you stay in the relationship, you might arrange for some sort of a transition, helping him stand on his own two feet.

After you have explored all your thoughts and feelings about what to do, let go of them and ask in your heart what the best choice is. When your heart has completed its process, you will know what to do.

HEALING THE RIP

You bonded with your boyfriend, and then, apparently for no reason, he broke up with you and ripped the bond. Your anger stems from this. To heal the rip, which is not unlike having something close to you destroyed or taken, it is helpful to recognize that the bond belonged as much to him as to you. He may have used that bond in a manner that was inconsiderate of you. Nonetheless, it was his right to choose. Under the circumstances, it probably would have been impossible for him to handle it differently.

COMPLEMENTARITY

There is much value occurring in both your lives individually and as a cooperative team. It is like a fugue, with two lines of music that spring from one theme but state it in different ways and relate to one another harmonically. You are each a statement of a musical theme complementing and contrasting one another, built upon a larger musical structure. When a pattern of energetic movement is built upon a greater symphonic accompaniment, there is indeed the potential for music that is profound and meaningful to many. Such an energetic pattern allows for a far richer release of impact than a duet that relates only to itself. In such a symphonic structure, there is much support for the individual parts. You experience greater intensity in your daily lives because of this connection to the symphonic whole. Things move more quickly and deeply.

PIONEERING

It is unfortunate that there are not many role models, nor much education, for having relationships based on higher values such as unconditional love and truth. Those seeking in this regard are pioneering, so there will be some stumbling, but it is certainly a worthy exploration. 🦜

Chapter 20

SEXUALITY
[Mostly to Specific Individuals]

SEX AND BALANCE

The greater the experience of inner balance and wholeness each partner has, the greater the opportunity to experience a larger wholeness through the sexual act. To the extent someone is seeking validation for himself from a sexual partner as opposed to already owning his validity, he is not free to reap from the sexual experience its larger harvest, a feast of shared aliveness.

Sex is a combining of energies that creates a new energy. Besides what you normally consider sex, this combining can occur between two or more people intellectually, emotionally, and spiritually. Lively conversation that leads to new understanding is an example of intellectual combining. People attending the theater or a gospel church service can experience an emotional combining of energies. Spiritual intercourse can be experienced in a group meditation.

Ideally, all these levels of intercourse occur to some degree during physical sex; even intellectual energies can be shared during sex, since words are not required for sharing intellectual energy. If you have been having intellectual, emotional, and spiritual intercourse with your partner in your relationship in general, you will tend to have them during sex.

EROS AND AGAPE

Is true love in the romantic sense eros or agape? Is agape romantic?

Romantic love is almost always eros, because it is attached to a particular person. You can also be in agape toward a person with whom you are romantically involved, so agape can be romantic. That rarely happens, but agape is the great goal.

HIGHER INTIMACY FIRST

Generally, most people do better if they do not have sex with a prospective mate until it springs from intimacy on other levels, until the love already shared is great enough to fill a physical expression of it.

We suggest that you enjoy whatever experiences come your way without holding onto them. You are still overly bothered by what might work out on a physical level with the people you come in contact with. We suggest instead tuning in to their inner qualities. That is where sex really occurs.

Let agape flood the other avenues of reality at your disposal. The physical will surely come along in due course.

BISEXUALITY AND HOMOSEXUALITY

Bisexuality and homosexuality are, of course, valid. Your soul has no gender. Each soul has varying percentages of male (focused) and female (creative) energy, but everyone has both male and female energies, and each soul can relate energetically to any other. The soul in this sense is bisexual—it can take either side in a creative act. This flexibility is the natural state of the universe. Whether or not you express this bisexuality through physical sex, everyone has the ability to relate in some way to both male and female energy, and must, if he is not to become one-sided. It is common for people to be physically bisexual to some degree in many of their lifetimes. In addition, virtually everyone will have at least one lifetime in which he is homosexual, because that is part of life on earth.

When you are in a male body, your primary lessons are about male energy, and in a female body, about female energy. However, the more lifetimes you have in both male and female bodies, the less your identity is limited to the sex of your present body. Therefore, you can use both your male and female energies as appropriate.

Satisfying sexual relationships are as you define them. All other things being equal, you have more balancing sex with someone of the opposite gender because, by definition, what is opposite is balancing. However, this does not invalidate sexual experiences with members of the same gender. If a sexual experience fulfills your particular needs and is satisfying to you, that is what matters. The choice to be heterosexual, homosexual, bisexual, or nonsexual is individual; there are no wrong choices. Every soul will choose each of those options at one time or another in order to experience growth.

On a scale of one to one hundred, with one hundred being the ultimate sexual experience, most people seldom if ever come close to one hundred. To reach the nineties, you would have to have ideal circumstances all the way around. If you reach the sixties, you will likely see that as being quite satisfying and pleasurable. Every element that could contribute to increased satisfaction does not have to be present.

You seem to imply that there is an element missing if you aren't with the opposite sex, that there is something about the physical male or female body itself.

The physical body has tendencies apart from the personality living in it. For example, a forty-year-old physical body tends to be most comfortable with others in approximately the same age range. Nevertheless, the person living in the body may feel differently, for whatever reasons, and nullify the body's tendency. For instance, he may have made an agreement before the lifetime to mate with someone who happens to be much older or younger than he is. Or, he may have unresolved issues that he can work out with an older or younger partner. Therefore, he is attracted to such partners.

There is much more to you than your physical body. You are the total of all your parts. This aspect of balance between opposite genders is just one element of many that can contribute to sexual satisfaction in a relationship. If it is missing because you are with someone of your own gender, there are many other elements that can bring satisfaction. It is not "wrong," and you may reach 70 on the scale even with that element missing. Someone who has that element but is missing many others may hit only 30.

Your sexual orientation was not specifically determined by your soul before your lifetime began; rather, you unconsciously chose it early in childhood at the same time you choose other key ideas on which to base your life. However, your soul can set up your life to point it in a certain direction through its choice of family dynamics and circumstances, among other things. Your life plan, which includes agreements and karmic debts to be repaid, can also make a particular choice of sexuality all but inevitable. Past life factors being worked on in the present lifetime also influence this choice. Nonetheless, the choice itself occurs on the level of personality, since the personality has free will. The personality usually ratifies the soul's influences, but it may not.

Some souls need same-sex relationships for internal balance. For example, those who have not been male frequently and who want to learn as much as they can about male energy might choose both to be born into a male body and to have sexual relationships with males as a way of reflecting their own experience back to them. Souls may also use homosexuality to learn to have loving relationships with the same sex if their same-sex relationships were often unloving in lifetimes when they were heterosexual. Those who persecuted homosexuals in a previous life may choose homosexuality as a way to learn compassion.

Often fixed homosexuality is a reaction to a culture's excessive polarization of the masculine and feminine. Like many other cultures, yours tend to see masculinity and femininity in terms of "either/or," rather than as two interrelated aspects of one thing on a continuum. They are promoted as extreme, limited, and rigid stereotypes rather than all-encompassing aspects of human potential. The softer qualities of manhood and the more focused qualities of womanhood are not adequately acknowledged and respected. Those who exhibit them are often seen as not being fully acceptable and are not allowed to simply be who they are.

At an early age, many children are given the message that they must fit into their gender's sexual stereotype. Boys often repress their softer traits, and girls, their more focused ones. This has begun to change in your society, but there is a long way to go. Young children who find their own gender's sexual stereotype unacceptable, unattainable, or both might identify with the other. This is often a factor in homosexuality.

Another factor can be unresolved rage toward the opposite sex. Where this is present, a child might reject that gender sexually. Of course, a child's relationship with his parents, as well as beliefs he carries over from past lifetimes, can influence his sexual orientation, so rage toward the opposite sex parent can be a dominant influence.

As with anything, those who choose same-sex orientation simply because they want to, because it will bring valuable lessons, rather than in reaction to external factors, tend to have an easier, more comfortable experience.

Many who classify themselves as being strictly heterosexual or homosexual are capable of bisexuality and might be more comfortable if that option were truly open in them, not necessarily for sexual intercourse, but at least for physically expressing affection. If their boundaries were not so rigid, they would have greater freedom to express love to others in whatever ways seem appropriate.

Any stimulation of the body in a pleasurable way can be construed as being sexual. This is why those who are homophobic sometimes have difficulty even hugging someone of the same sex. A hug can be pleasurable, and that brings up fears that they are being sexual with a member of the same sex. Having such rigid definitions of one's sexuality is not conducive to loving relationships. We encourage openness, letting your experience be whatever it naturally is.

SEX ON HIGHER PLANES

Is there an equivalent of sex on other planes, and if so, can you describe it?

Sexual intercourse on higher planes becomes increasingly intense, powerful, and inclusive of more essences. Sex can be defined as a blending of energies. From the standpoint of higher planes, it could be asked if sex exists on the physical plane, because your experience of it is so limited. However, it is what you can handle. ⚘

Chapter 21

RELATIONSHIPS AND POWER

Mature relationships generate and expand power. We are not referring merely to sexual relationships. Any type of relationship is potentially powerful.

On higher planes of existence, there is much more direct experience of power. This is possible because of the skills developed earlier on the physical plane in relationships. Relationships give you a variety of ways to learn how to know another person. Since every person is part of the whole, each relationship gives you an opportunity to know more about the whole. The more you know how to know another person, and the more you know about the whole, the more you are able to generate power in relationships. Whether you have joy or pain in a relationship, it can always teach you something about this.

The best dancers have great sensitivity to one another. It is not enough to learn the steps. Someone can be excellent as a solo dancer but be relatively poor with a partner because of a lack of empathy. It does not matter whether you are leading or following; just as the one who is following must be responsive to the one who is leading, the one who is leading must be sensitive to the one who is following. Otherwise, his movements may be arbitrary, crude, or imposing.

Although a mature relationship generates power, most relationships are not about that yet; they are about learning how to dance without stepping on one another's toes too often. Many times one or both of the partners hobble away from the dance with bloody bandages on their feet, if not a cast all the way up their legs. In such relationships there is not much real relating. Relating requires clearly communicating your thoughts and feelings, and empathy, the ability to receive another's thoughts and feelings. All relationships give you opportunities to practice both skills.

Generally, the more experiences you have had, both in the present lifetime and in past lives, the more empathy you have.

You know from your own background what it is like to walk in others' shoes. You may need to be reminded from time to time—we all do—but if you have been there before, it comes back to you. When you have empathy, you desire not to bring pain to another, because you know what his pain feels like from your own experience. You can also gain empathy by being open to understanding someone else's experience even if it has not been your own. For instance, whenever you lock horns with someone and then come to understand his point of view, you have gained a wider perspective and richer empathy.

Sometimes people lament that nobody understands them. However, it is your responsibility to communicate yourself clearly to others. Maybe they still will not understand, but that is not the issue until you have communicated clearly. It takes thought to do this. Sometimes people try to make themselves clear by saying more, covering every possible detail that comes to mind, but that is usually confusing. Fewer well-chosen words communicate more clearly than many poorly chosen ones.

On the foundation of empathy and clear communication, it is possible to come into alignment and agreement with another person. Alignment relates to an affinity of purpose. Two people are aligned when they seek the same or complementary things. For example, two people are aligned when both are focused on spiritual growth, or on becoming as rich as they possibly can. If one person has a desire to serve his country and his partner wants to serve him so that he can serve his country, they are aligned through having complementary purposes. An example of lack of alignment is one person wanting money above all, and the other, spiritual growth.

Sometimes people who were in alignment no longer are because their priorities have changed. In such a case, it may be sensible to part and move on. Occasionally couples who are not in alignment have a relationship similar to a business deal— they each get something they want out of it. There is nothing wrong with this, but it is not a powerful relationship. Also, if there is deception, and especially self-deception, about the true nature of the relationship, it is likely to break down.

Agreement is generated out of alignment. If two people are in alignment because they each value spiritual growth most highly, they may not yet have come into agreement about the means to achieve it. One of them might feel that meditating for two hours every day is the best way. The other might feel that it is more important to spend those two hours volunteering in a shelter for the homeless. They have alignment but not agreement, especially if each is trying to convince the other that his way is right. Through empathy and communication, they can negotiate an agreement. They might agree, for example, to alternate between meditating and volunteering. Or, they might simply agree that each of them is free to do what he feels is right for himself.

People's needs are continually changing. Every relationship needs to be readjusted through negotiation from time to time, to ensure that it is working well for everyone involved. You might assume that your partner still agrees to something to which he once agreed. Furthermore, you might assume that your partner agreed to something to which he never did. So it is well to check in from time to time and see where things stand.

When there is empathy and clear communication, negotiation is not long and drawn-out, or the constant focus of the relationship. Ideally, relationships are primarily devoted to joyful and productive sharing. However, if there is a problem, there may be a need to negotiate some new agreements. Anything in a relationship can be negotiated. It is helpful to enter negotiations having prioritized your needs and given creative thought to ways of meeting them.

A healthy, powerful relationship is one in which there is alignment and agreement built on empathy and clear communication. A healthy relationship can promote physical health. Sex, for example, can be a potent means of generating health-giving power. Where empathy and communication skills are weak, misunderstandings, deceptions, or undealt-with issues can enter in, damaging whatever alignment and agreement there is. As a result, the relationship's power decreases, and a person's individual power may be drained. That can lead to physical illness.

People lacking in empathy and communication skills are often inclined to blame the other person for the failure of a relationship, or feel that somehow, the love just died. They may keep repeating the pattern with others until they recognize the problem. Those who are promiscuous may generate more power sexually with those whom they do not know well than in a relationship; they have a "clean slate" each time, and some alignment based on attraction. They may experience more power than those who are monogamous in a long-term relationship that is "dead." However, when a couple increases its alignment and agreement through empathy and communication, the power generated through sex and through the entire relationship can multiply well beyond what is experienced by either those in a "dead" relationship or those who are promiscuous.

Empathy and clear communication in a relationship allow any subject to be appropriately discussed. Clear communication springs from neutrality. Neutrality does not mean being blasé and feelingless. However, it is without excess charge and hidden agendas. In neutrality, you simply state facts and feelings as they are for you, not to hurt or impose, but to inform and share.

If you have excess charge about an issue that would distort your communication, it is a good idea to work the charge out first. For example, if you have anger out of proportion to what triggered it, old, unresolved anger is coming up along with the new. You can work out the old anger by venting it physically. You might consciously release your anger as you pound a pillow, chop some wood, or do some vigorous exercise. Then you are in a better position to be neutral and communicate your anger clearly and fairly.

The way to fulfillment in relationships is to give fully what is in your heart, with accuracy and sensitivity, whether it is your affection, concerns, or anger. Once you have done this in your life, you cannot go back to withholding. This does not impose on others. Nevertheless, if your partner is withholding, he is likely to experience it as pressure to open. If he chooses not to, in time your relationship is likely to end. You would then tend to attract those who are interested in giving fully.

In a powerful relationship, two people share the joy of being themselves in a multiplication of energy. ❦

Part 6

COMMUNION

❧ Chapter 22 ❧

ESSENCE CONTACT

Essence contact occurs when the personality opens to its essence or to the essence of another. It brings growth and joy, and if the opening is great enough, ecstasy, even if the contact only lasts a moment. Brief essence contact gives some indication of what is possible when barriers are finally eliminated. Essence contact can occur with any essence, incarnate or otherwise.

The most important essence contact is with yourself. You cannot contact another's essence more deeply than you contact your own. There are many aspects of self, but the source of self is your essence, so knowing your essence is crucial to knowing yourself. It is not hard to love yourself when you know yourself, especially your essence.

Most people fear essence contact and consequently have had a very limited experience of it, if any at all, because false personality (the fear-based ego) is dissolved in essence. If you go deeply enough into your essence, you reach the Tao itself, for your essence is cast from the Tao.

Is there a letdown or hangover, so to speak, after ecstasy, or a greater experience beyond ecstasy?

When you open to your essence, you feel empowered. Because essence contact accelerates your growth and deepens your connection with yourself, old fears may surface in the aftermath. Nevertheless, you also feel greater strength with which to deal with them, although you might need some outside assistance as well.

You often experience ecstasy when you leave your body as you sleep, but because the waking personality is not equipped to deal with it (ecstasy does not fit into its landscape), the personality blocks the memory of it.

You will not allow yourself to experience more than you are ready for. Perhaps in holding eye contact for a moment with someone you care about, you experience essence contact. Although it is very pleasing, a moment may be all you can handle. Maybe next time you will be able to handle two moments.

Whenever you open to yourself—thinking about yourself in a newly loving way, for instance, or seeing yourself as you never have before—you make essence contact more readily available.

There are degrees of openness to your essence, and it is always possible to open more. When you increase your openness a great deal at once, you feel an ecstatic "rush" of expansion. When you get used to a particular level of openness to your essence, it no longer feels like ecstasy in the sense of something explosive or revelatory. However, your everyday level would be experienced as ecstasy by someone accustomed to a much lower level, if he opened to it all at once. It would tax his capabilities to open that wide. It would be thrilling yet frightening at the same time. Even if it were momentary, it would bring much growth. He would remember, at least unconsciously, how it felt and would have something new to work toward. He might resist it, because such a change in function would require much of him. The false personality is devoted to the status quo, but the essence seeks ecstasy, so we all eventually keep moving.

Essence contact requires coming fully into the present moment. When you "plug in" to the socket of the present moment, the circuit completes, energy moves, and the light comes on; you "get it." You see the impact of the moment. You see who you are, and who the other person is, if it involves another person.

Does the personality fall away upon plugging in to essence?

No. It becomes enlightened. The light comes on; the personality becomes light as opposed to heavy. In other words, it becomes the true personality rather than the false personality. In enlightenment, all parts of the personality become open to receive and transmit love. Think of a neon sign as representing the personality. Not plugged in or turned on, the sign can be rather dingy. Its true colors do not show, and it may even be an eyesore. Turn it on, and it looks totally different. You can see it from several blocks away. This is what essence contact does.

Two people who "fall in love" with each other may momentarily put aside their fears about intimacy and allow essence contact. There have been many things written about the way people who are in love glow. If you "fall in love" with yourself, you can have a similar experience. Your relationships with both others and yourself can teach you much about developing and sustaining essence contact. Allowing barriers to fall and improving communication can help provide a stable foundation upon which essence contact can happen more regularly and deeply. However, that is not the essence contact itself. Essence contact with another person often happens seemingly by accident. Sometimes you both just happen to find yourselves in the present moment and before you can stop it, there you are, in contact!

Is there a realistic limit to striving for essence contact?

The limit is how much you are willing to be conscious. Some people find it too much trouble. Even those who remain mostly unconscious may have some essence contact, and therefore, growth. However, the growth is more laborious, painful, and slow than when there is conscious opening to your essence. ❧

ॐ **Chapter 23** ॐ

ONENESS

For many people, it is frightening to contemplate the dissolution of their separateness. This fear often stands in the way of achieving emotional intimacy with another person. Many people are afraid that they will lose themselves if they open that much.

If you find that in opening, you lose yourself, you are not experiencing true oneness. In a romantic relationship in which one partner loses himself in the other, what is really going on? Usually the one losing himself does not have a strong sense of identity to begin with. The relationship is begun with a premise such as, "I am nothing and you are something. I am weak and you are strong; you will make me safe." The other person becomes the identity for the one losing himself. In your culture, it has been more common for women to do this than for men. This is symbolized by the fact that until recently, women who married inevitably lost their last names. We are not saying that women should always keep their own last names when they marry; that is a matter of choice—it might be more convenient to change the name. What is important is how it is viewed.

Although oneness is the truth, whether you know it or not, it is not necessarily wise to try to have an experience of total oneness all at once. It is not possible anyway. To experience oneness, you must first have a strong sense of self. You need the knowledge that you are safe, that you are who you are no matter what.

Before you decided to take this great journey on earth, you were in a state of total oneness, a spark of the Tao. To expand the Tao's awareness and creativity, you cast part of yourself into the dimensional universe and began your present cycle of exploration.

Some experience of separateness and isolation is appropriate and inevitable on the physical plane, because this plane is designed to allow you to explore who you individually are as a unique being. The physical body's solid boundary reinforces the experience of separateness. When this experience is appropriate, you take it for granted; you do not question or worry about it. When it is excessive or unnecessary, loneliness results. If you are willing to help others and allow them to help you, much loneliness can be eliminated.

When a soul first incarnates on the physical plane, having just come from the Tao, he still has a strong sense of oneness. He is like an infant who still largely feels like part of his mother. As the soul matures, he goes through a phase in which he learns to assert his individuality, like a child establishing his own identity. This is the time of maximum separateness. After that, the soul moves again toward an experience of oneness. However, it is now conscious oneness. The soul develops a larger and larger perspective based on his experience, just as a child does as he grows up. The amount of isolation that felt natural when he was asserting his individuality would now feel excessive and would result in loneliness. The experience of separation becomes starkly visible against the sensing of how lovely it would be to open again to the greater universe of which he is becoming more aware.

Loneliness is an important feeling, because it causes you to seek oneness, seek to open your encasement of isolation. A knight's armor protected him from mortal wounds in battle. However, afterward, it was apt to feel mighty uncomfortable, perhaps hot, since it did not breathe. At some point he would feel ready to take it off. Loneliness is like the knight's discomfort in his armor.

People often assume that having other people around will ensure an end to loneliness. If you have not opened, other people will not end your loneliness. Other people may help you open, but if you interact with people who do not nurture you, you may want to close down even more. The answer to loneliness is not primarily in finding the right mate, going to a party, or whatever; it is in opening to oneness.

Those who have been deeply wounded emotionally, either in this lifetime or in recent prior lives, may expect harm and therefore find it more difficult to open. When you are on the physical plane, there is always the possibility of harm, from either yourself or others. A thick encasement cannot truly protect you; neither can you create a situation for yourself on the physical plane that is guaranteed to be completely safe. However, it is not necessary to do so. Every organism can sustain a certain amount of harm, recover, and move on. The excessive fear of harm comes from a belief that you are weak and fragile, and hence cannot tolerate virtually any harm. If you wish to open, the first step is to change that belief and rediscover the strength you have. This might entail taking some sort of apparently risky action that changes your life situation, proving to yourself that you have the power to do this. An example is speaking up to someone with whom you have had a tendency to hold back.

Some people also find it difficult to open because of a fear of being seen. They believe that they are bad somehow and that others will see this—their guilty secrets, or what is wrong or inadequate about them, will be exposed. However, opening to oneness primarily reveals the glorious eternal being you are.

"Self-made millionaires" often take many risks and fail, but have the courage to keep trying new ideas until they succeed. Those who are successful on the spiritual path are also generally marked by a high level of courage. They are willing to take calculated risks when they do not know how things will turn out. They move forward, sometimes even trembling from head to toe, not knowing if they will be smashed under the boots of the "giant."

You will have the ultimate experience of oneness when your journey is over and you are fully reunited with the Tao, which has total consciousness of oneness. The Tao, in a sense, is not differentiated or fragmented. It is one whole, even though each part is valid as a part. There is complete integration, in other words, and hence oneness is the natural experience. As you journey back to the Tao, you experience increasing oneness.

There is a right amount of openness for you. You do not have to force anything. If you open as much as you can, you will probably be able to open a little more next time—there is a continual increase. It might be compared to stretching tight shoes. A shoemaker's stretching machine gently and gradually stretches the leather as it is able to give. If the machine were to push too hard, it would rip the leather. Your essence is characterized by love, and love does not impose; love is infinitely strong, so it can afford to be infinitely gentle. Your essence knows that it is eternal, and that eventually all encasements will dissolve when they are no longer needed or wanted.

Ironically, the more you experience oneness, the more your individuality is enhanced. Not only do you not lose yourself—you find yourself. By letting go to what is beyond you, you are also letting go to who you are, because you are letting go of your encasement. If you have no encasement, you are free to share with others in any way that is appropriate.

We, the Michael entity, are 1050 souls who blend on a continual basis in a way that is incomprehensible to you on the physical plane. It is not yet total oneness, but we experience a relatively high degree of oneness with one another, and with others as well. We work together like the cells of an organism. If the cells in your body are healthy, they are one with all the other cells, particularly those around them. They exchange substances on a continual basis. Cells have walls, but not encasements. The walls are permeable and there is right relationship with what is around them. The fact that there is oneness does not cause the cells to lose their individuality; a brain cell is different from a skin cell. They all function, though, as part of the same larger whole: the body.

Oneness is not merely the absence of an encasement. It is an active connectedness to the All, the ability of the part to give and receive freely into the whole. For many, the first step on the spiritual path is to learn how to give. They practice being selfless Good Samaritans. This may be helpful in breaking down their encasements. The second step for them might be to learn how to receive. There are those who can give but cannot receive. If a cell gave but did not receive, it would soon be empty and would implode. If it received but did not give, it would eventually absorb more than it could handle and would explode. The healthy cell both gives and receives without obstruction. The highest spiritual state is not to give or to receive dominantly, but to be permeable, to be constantly both giving and receiving. This is a state that could be called being. You are a human being—you are designed to both give and receive simultaneously.

Giving is not the same as imposing: "I'm going to give this to you whether you like it or not, for your own good." Likewise, receiving is not the same as taking: "I want this for me; you can't have it." You only feel the need to impose when you are encased. When you experience oneness, you know that you and everyone else are already part of all things.

MEDITATION

See the encasements you use to make yourself safe. Thank them for what they have provided you. Explore whether you still need them. If not, let them dissolve. ☜

❧ Chapter 24 ❧

BLENDING

Sharing benefits everyone who truly participates in it. A teacher, if he is truly teaching, gains as much as those he teaches. If a teacher is merely imparting information rather than participating in a process with his students, he may not benefit very much. The students may or may not benefit, depending on the quality of the information and its usefulness in their lives. Such a teacher may feel that he is standing on a mountaintop of superior knowledge, and distributing some of his intellectual largesse, either out of the goodness of his heart, or for the paycheck, or for other forms of gratification. But he would probably not say that he is truly benefiting from the act of teaching itself.

This is an example that applies to all interactions. In a marriage, for example, if one partner seems to be getting more than the other, there is not, at least to that extent, a true inter-change or sharing. One of them may feel that he is standing on a mountaintop of greater love, time, money, or energy. One partner may be on a particular kind of mountaintop, and the other on a different kind: "I give you more of this, and you give me more of that." In that case, it is more like a business deal than the intercourse of two souls. There is nothing wrong with this; whatever people choose to create in their lives is a valid learning experience. However, where there is true intercourse, there is no superiority and inferiority. In true sharing between two people, one is not doing something *at* the other. It is a state of being together.

You cannot share with another any more deeply than you have plumbed in yourself. If part of you is not available to yourself, it is not available to be shared. If you have gone much more deeply into yourself than your partner has, the depth to which your partner has gone is the limit of your possible shar-ing. Of course, it is not cut-and-dried. You may have gone more deeply in certain areas, and your partner may have gone more deeply in others. In whatever area you are sharing, the one who has gone less deeply establishes your limits. It is not necessarily negative that there are limits on what can be shared. In fact, there are always limits on what can be shared. Furthermore, you are not likely to be interested in sharing as deeply with a store clerk as with your mate; yet something can be shared with the clerk.

Many people do not even notice clerks. They do something at them, such as give them money so they can make their purchases. Of course, often clerks are not interested in sharing with their customers either. But if you are willing to share in whatever way is possible, and the clerk is also open to it, you can each share something of yourself.

Most human beings are lonely to some extent. There is a deep sense of loss because of the knowledge on some level of what could be shared that is not. You must be brave to risk possible hurt when you open to others. Such bravery, though, is not heroic; it is practical, since the alternative is no sharing.

You might say that the physical plane is the elementary school of blending. Blending is a sharing of energies; it is the highest form of sharing. Sharing in other ways makes blending possible. You learn blending through sharing in relationships with others.

Your primary relationship is with yourself. You are multi-faceted; getting to know yourself is a very lengthy process. You come to know yourself not only through inner contemplation, but through your intercourse with other people—including store clerks. What you are becomes illuminated when interacting with what you are not, which is to say, other people, for the most part. When you learn about yourself through intercourse with what you are not, you discover that what you are not is also what you are. In other words, you are part of all with which you interact, and everything is part of one whole; the parts reveal the whole. Coming to more fully know who you and others are as individuals is how you come to know the whole in its specificity. You can have a sense of oneness in general, and that can be pleasant, but you do not know the whole until you know yourself. And you do not know yourself until you have developed the ability to share with others.

Fear inevitably builds walls that prevent sharing. In self-deprecation, which is a fear of being inadequate, you distance yourself from others by viewing them as superior. On the other hand, in arrogance, a fear of being vulnerable, you distance yourself by viewing others as inferior. In martyrdom, a fear of being unworthy, you view others as persecutors, which, of course, likewise distances you. In stubbornness, a fear of change, you dig in your heels and hold your ground, which is certainly not conducive to the fluid dance that is blending. And so forth. As you work on eliminating such traits in yourself, you automatically learn how to blend more. If, for example, you start to catch yourself believing the lie that others are superior to you, you can assert the truth that everyone is equal. This will help you interact with others more and more freely, because they begin to look approachable.

Sexual intercourse is an excellent opportunity for blending. When sex is not fulfilling, often it is because one person is doing something *to* the other, or both are doing something to each other, rather than there being an exchange—they are not letting each other in, and not moving out to each other. You cannot understand another person unless you blend with him.

Perhaps the most common human interaction is conversation. Even so, how little listening there is! Listening allows the other person in. By the same token, the one speaking must be willing to reveal himself to the one listening if there is to be blending. It is a two-way street, as they say. Conversation in which blending occurs is quite fulfilling.

On higher planes of existence, blending is much less restricted. First of all, there are no physical bodies to broadcast the illusion of separateness. Also, there is little fear on higher planes; since there are no physical bodies, there are no threats to physical survival, which is at the root of most human fears. However, what you can share on the astral plane, when you are between lifetimes or after you complete your series of lifetimes, is largely dependent on what you learn about sharing on the physical plane. Because it is more challenging on the physical plane, you have the opportunity to learn it well. Although it is made more difficult than it really needs to be, if it were too easy you would be likely to take many aspects of the process for granted. You cannot do on higher planes what you can do here; that is why you are here.

By the way, when we say "higher," we do not mean better. A higher plane is simply one that vibrates at a faster speed. Those on higher planes are not necessarily any smarter than you are. They are merely in a different stage of development. But the higher the plane, the more thorough and encompassing the blending tends to be.

In blending on higher planes, you totally feel the vibration of another essence. It is like sex without a physical body, only much more intense and pleasurable.

Every essence is unique. If essences were compared to flavors, the universe could be compared to a gigantic ice cream parlor with an infinite number of delicious flavors. Blending is a way to experience flavors other than your own. Some people, when beginning to learn to blend, choose to blend only with those who are very much like themselves. That is safer, it seems, and is actually a good way to learn to know and love yourself; loving someone who is like yourself reinforces your own sense of being lovable. But those who are more adventurous like to blend with a wide variety of flavors, and feel safe in doing so because they know that they will not lose who they are. They have practiced sharing enough to have proven this to themselves. This blending can occur in any department of life, not just during physical sex.

All people have aspects of themselves that are not yet healthy. Some hold back from blending out of shame, but blending facilitates healing. An example is feeling better after bringing a "deep, dark secret" into the open with someone you trust. When you allow yourself to blend with others, you find that you are a beautiful soul, part of the All That Is. In addition, when you share deeply with another, new aspects of yourself come forth, because there is a place for them to be received.

You sometimes find yourself saying things, for example, that you did not know that you knew; you are amazed at your profundity and wisdom!

All creation is a result of blending. Babies and universes alike are born from the blending of the male and female principles. Even something you created apparently by yourself is the result of blending: different parts of your consciousness blend, and something new is born. Blending is expansive; it imparts a radiant glow that attracts others, both physical and nonphysical, and invites support and larger blending. The nonphysical support and blending sometimes result in what is called inspiration. So blending leads to more blending, creativity to more creativity, and sharing to more sharing, until the limits forged by fear stop the process. At that point, you have a golden opportunity to examine the fear and let it go.

If little blending is happening in your life, internally or externally, start from where you are and do what you can do. To get the ball rolling, start sharing with others in little ways. Look for the opportunities inherent in all your situations; do not write anyone off. If you are in a relationship that feels stuck, do not blame it on your partner, saying, "Well, I'm willing to share, but my partner isn't, or hasn't plumbed the depths inside himself that I have." There is usually something you can share with any human being—find that something. Explore in yourself what might be standing in your way. The adventure of blending is the adventure of being. It is the productive activity of every plane of being, until you return to the Tao, where you are totally blended with everything. If you are not blending, you are, you might say, unemployed, which is not very satisfying.

The capability of blending with all things is agape: unconditional, total love. In agape, you look at everything and say, "This is me." You experience complete unification. You are not expected to have this experience in its totality now, on the physical plane, but it is the great goal; it is what you are working toward. If you wish to be spiritually richer, expand your capacity to love. This is done by blending.

Since you cannot blend with another beyond what is available in yourself, self-forgiveness is essential. Self-judgment imprisons the parts of yourself you have labeled "bad." Self-forgiveness releases them, making more of yourself available for blending. Self-forgiveness results from clarifying your understanding. When you clearly see the reasons you did something or developed a certain way of being, forgiveness comes automatically. You realize that your destructive traits did not spring from an inherent "badness" in you. Also, when you see the traits clearly, you can change them. You cannot change anything about yourself before you see it clearly and understand its reasons for being.

Until you have true understanding, you are a prisoner of your own misconceptions. You may try to fix something that is not broken, and not fix something that is. You cannot see yourself clearly, forgive yourself, and make changes without loving yourself. If you hate yourself, your subconscious will not reveal itself to you.

You can see this with children who "misbehave." If you are loving toward a child and he trusts you, he will likely tell you why he did something, and you have a means of correcting the situation. If you take a hateful, accusatory approach toward him, he will likely hide his true reasons to try to protect himself, or he may form destructive patterns in order to cope with you.

EXERCISE

To learn to love yourself more, think of someone else whom you love very much, and what that feels like. Then project those feelings toward yourself.

Love starts with the premise that you are good; hate starts with the premise that you are bad. When you understand how things are, you can only start with the premise that you are good. You are a part of the All. Every human being has done violent and destructive things that have hurt others, in past lives if not in this one. However, destructive actions are not a result of being bad, but of being ignorant. When you understand, you can function at a higher level.

How do you deal with someone who refuses to be open?

Everyone has some area of openness, or he would not be alive. The only practical solution with someone who is mostly closed is to share whatever small amount to which he is open. If you would like to share "this much" but he would only like to share "that much," allow "that much" to be as beautiful and free a sharing as it can be. If you fill "that much" full, it will start to expand. It may never expand to the size you would like, but you might as well accept the best that is possible in that situation. Hopefully, others in your life fill in the gaps.

You cannot force another person to open and share. However, sharing, when it is happening freely, is a wonderful experience. The joy of it can be contagious.

MEDITATION

See yourself blending with all the parts of yourself.
See yourself blending with other important people in your life.
See yourself blending with all humanity.
See all humanity blending with the entire earth, including its
    atmosphere.
See the earth blending with the entire solar system.
See the solar system blending with the universe.
See the universe blending with the Tao.
See yourself blending with the Tao.
Bask in the knowledge of oneness such blending brings.

Blending, when allowed to blossom to its full capacity, brings unspeakable joy. 🍃

ABOUT THE AUTHOR

SHEPHERD HOODWIN is a Laguna Beach, California channel, workshop leader, and teacher. He does counseling, past-life therapy, and channeling coaching, in addition to both individual and group channeling sessions and intuitive readings. He is the author of several articles on the Michael teachings and six books of channeled material, including *The Journey of Your Soul—A Channel Explores Channeling and the Michael Teachings* and *Meditations for Self-Discovery— Guided Journeys for Communicating with Your Inner Self,* as well as an upcoming children's book, *Sabina and the Angels' Golden Crystals.* He has been channeling Michael since 1986. He is a graduate of the University of Oregon in Music Education, and is a songwriter, singer, and actor. He is currently writing a musical.

GLOSSARY

Agape: A state of unconditional love for everything. This is considered the highest goal. (Usually pronounced *ah*-guh-pay.)

Astral plane: Where we go between lifetimes and when we are finished with the physical plane.

Causal plane: The next plane after the astral. Michael's plane of creation.

Entity: Usually refers to a "spiritual family" of about 1000 souls. Michael is the name of one particular entity.

Essence: Soul, or "higher" self, in distinction to the outer personality, or "lower" self.

False personality: False ego, the part of self motivated by fear.

Planes of creation: Physical, astral, causal, akashic, mental, messianic, and buddhaic. Just as there are seven colors in the rainbow and seven steps in a musical scale, each with a different vibratory rate, there are seven levels of being on the spectrum of creation. The slowest speed of vibration is on the physical plane; the highest, on the buddhaic plane. From there, universal substance returns to the Tao.

Physical plane: The densest of the seven planes, where we presently reside.

Soul: Essence, or "higher" self, in distinction to the outer personality, or "lower" self.

Tao: The All That Is. Usually refers to the dimensionless ground of being rather than to its expression in the seven planes of creation of the manifest universe. [See Planes of creation.] Michael normally uses the word *Tao* in place of *God* (depending on the beliefs of those listening) because *God* is usually personified and tends to connote something hierarchical and judgmental. They sometimes also use the word *God* to signify the overall consciousness of the manifest universe.

OTHER SUMMERJOY PRESS BOOKS
By Shepherd Hoodwin

NOTE: All in-print Michael and Summerjoy Press books can be ordered through any bookstore or from Summerjoy Press, 31423 S. Coast Hwy. #84, Laguna Beach CA 92677-3056, 888-LIVE JOY (888-548-3569). Volume discounts on Summerjoy Press books are available from the publisher, as is information about upcoming Summerjoy books and cassettes, and private sessions and workshops with Shepherd Hoodwin.

THE JOURNEY OF YOUR SOUL—A Channel Explores Channeling and the Michael Teachings

This 419-page book is the most in-depth discussion of the Michael teachings to date. It may also be the first analytical study of channeling written by a channel. It has a foreword by Jon Klimo, the author of *Channeling: Investigations on Receiving Information from Paranormal Sources* (Jeremy P. Tarcher, Inc., Los Angeles, 1987). Klimo writes, *"The Journey of Your Soul* may well be the best (Michael) book of them all due to its clarity, thoroughness, and detail, and thanks to the fact that the author, an exceptionally clear-headed Michael channel himself, brings real integrity and authenticity to our understanding of Michael in particular and to the channeling process in general."

MEDITATIONS FOR SELF-DISCOVERY—Guided Journeys for Communicating with Your Inner Self

This is a beautiful collection of forty-five vivid, often pastoral, guided imagery meditations channeled from Shepherd's essence (higher self). There are many meditation cassettes available, but this is one of the first collections of meditations in book form that can be read to oneself or to others. Teachers and anyone who leads groups would find it particularly useful. It would also be cherished as a gift book. It includes blank pages for journaling.

REVIEWS AND FURTHER TESTIMONIALS FOR
LOVING FROM YOUR SOUL

People everywhere are seeking a higher perspective on love than the popular view of romance. This outstanding new book goes to the core of the issue by illuminating the nature of love as a reality that is always available. Received from the Michael entity and written with vibrant clarity, *Loving from Your Soul* will have a resounding impact on the way we look at love from now on.
 —*Leading Edge Review*

This collection of material from lectures and private "Michael channeling sessions" explores the nature of love itself—what is love, and what is it to love and be loved. Full of wisdom and inspiration and touching on some of our favorite topics—expanding love, loving yourself, friendship, abundance, and essence contact—*Loving from Your Soul* is an excellent guide for new paradigm lovers of any persuasion.
 —Deborah Anapol, Ph.D., *Loving More* magazine

I just finished reading *Loving from Your Soul*. It was so healing—excellent!
 —C.D., Sarasota, Florida

Loving from Your Soul has been a great help—I refer to it all the time.
 —L.O., Michigan City, Indiana

I found *Loving from Your Soul* to be sound, informative, redemptive—a near-perfect book.
 —B.W., Knox, Indiana